AF255471

# Who is My Neighbor?

# Who is My Neighbor?

Adam C. Sikorski, DMin

WIPF *&* STOCK · Eugene, Oregon

WHO IS MY NEIGHBOR?



Wipf & Stock
An Imprint of Wipf and Stock Publishers
199 W. 8th Ave., Suite 3
Eugene, OR 97401

www.wipfandstock.com

PAPERBACK ISBN: 978-1-6667-5900-6
HARDCOVER ISBN: 978-1-6667-5901-3
EBOOK ISBN: 978-1-6667-5902-0

Scripture taken from the New American Standard Bible, Copyright 1960, 1962, 1963, 1968, 1971, 1972, 1973, 1975, 1977 by The Lockman Foundation. Used by permission. All right reserved.

Edited by Lois E. Olena

# Dedication

This book is dedicated to everyone in the church community. It is my desire that this book will be the catalytic event in your life that propels you to actions. I believe the local church is the hope of the world, therefore we must do everything we can to engage and understand our neighbor.

# Contents

# Preface

As American culture continues to morph, pastors face different complexities. The cultural climate in America today presents polarizing subject matter, manifested as societal pressures that divide communities and impact families and churches. One of the main divisive issues is the topic of race and racism. To effectively minister to diverse people in American communities, current and future pastors must increase in cultural competency; unfortunately, many pastors do not know what steps to take to even embark on the quest.

This book came about as a result of my doctoral research, which utilized the Intercultural Development Inventory (IDI) to leverage a key learning opportunity for five vocational ministry students at North Central University in Minneapolis, Minnesota, guiding them toward increasing their cultural competency. The IDI assessment provided metrics that pinpointed specific areas of growth, in addition to providing a baseline to measure current and future culturally competent growth. Students navigated eight sessions framed around the IDI's Ten Key Intercultural Learning Opportunities. Results documented ranged from increased self-awareness to catalytic events, providing a framework for current and future pastors desiring to increase their cultural competency.

Because this research was founded on strong biblical-theological principles and utilized effective professional resources and tools for increasing cultural competency, I chose to make it available to pastors and ministry leaders. Ultimately, anyone with an open heart and an awareness of the Holy Spirit can move toward an increased cultural competency in order to deal with racism, which only fosters disunity, and more effectively reach out to diverse populations in local communities.

# Acknowledgments

First and foremost, I want to thank my wife, Stacy, who endured years of me attending seminary; perhaps one could argue that she also earned a degree through the process. Nonetheless, her unending support and consistent encouragement fueled me more than she will ever know. She has been the consummate cheerleader, spurring me on even when I wanted to give up. To my children Reghan and Keghan: I always attempted to balance work and play, but I know, at times, I came up short. Thank you for your grace and mercy. I love you all more than words can describe.

I cannot express enough gratitude to my parents. I would not be where I am today had they not encouraged me every step of the way. They always believed in me and encouraged me to pursue God's call on my life. They taught me to hear God's voice and to have the courage to respond to what God is speaking. Their unwavering love and support made me a better person.

While in third grade, I was introduced to a person, who happened to be my gym teacher. This person would later become my youth pastor and have an extremely profound impact on my life. Edgar Cabello will never know the amount of love and appreciation I have for him. He always stuck with me through thick and thin and always saw potential in my life. Thank you for calling out that potential and thank you for always believing in me.

The city of Detroit will always hold a special place in my heart. When God was nudging me toward urban ministry, it was the one place I did not want to go. Nevertheless, God had other plans. Never could I imagine that my time at Revival Tabernacle, under the tutelage of Pastor Tim Dilena, would become so foundational for my spiritual development. The devotional habits that I employ today are the direct result of Pastor Tim's influence and example. Additionally, I am eternally grateful to the pastors and parishioners of Revival Tabernacle. You provided the catalytic event in my life that birthed my doctoral work and ultimately this book.

To the faculty and staff at the Assemblies of God Theological Seminary (AGTS), I cannot adequately express my appreciation for your support and encouragement. The assistance of DMin Project Coordinator,

Dr. Lois Olena, was instrumental for the completion of this book. Also, I extend a special "thank you" to Dr. Charlie Self. I am sure he does not remember the phone conversation, but I do. That conversation changed the trajectory of my doctoral path. Thank you for speaking life into my passions and thank you for always modeling leadership through humility.

North Central University has some amazing faculty and staff. While there is not enough space to thank everyone, I do want to specifically mention a few people. First, to the former president, Dr. Gordon Anderson, thank you for opening the door for me to return to my alma mater; it was a dream come true. As an undergrad student at NCU, I always looked up to you. You inspired me in my educational pursuits, and you inspired me to be a Pentecostal leader. I will always remember my first chapel as a faculty member sitting on stage watching you speak. All I could do was sit there and smile. Second, the T. J. Jones Library on the NCU campus was my home away from home during my doctoral work. Thank you, Judy Pruitt, and Jordan Kleinschmidt, for your help with acquiring countless books, which aided my research. I could not have completed the work without your assistance.

Finally, I would like to thank my doctoral project adviser, Dr. Mark Hausfeld, and my biblical adviser, Dr. Jac Perrin, for their assistance and advice. I appreciate their sacrifice of time and energy to read through the countless pages.

I am eternally grateful for everyone who has directly and indirectly impacted and influenced my doctoral work as well as this book— the culmination of everyone's significant contributions in my life.

# Introduction

Although the racial divide in America has decreased since the abolishment of slavery, events in the past ten years demonstrate that racial inequality still exists. The church has an opportunity to lead the way when it comes to bridging that racial divide. Unfortunately, racial disparity is glaringly obvious within local churches. While racial issues are not new within American culture, exposure to the ramifications is unprecedented in human history. As a result, racial issues continue to produce a polarizing effect on the broader American culture.

As the demographics of the U.S. continue to change, many sources have attempted to project future demographic shifts within the country. While various reports issue different numbers, a common denominator exists that within the near future, Caucasian Americans will no longer be the majority in the country.[1] Unfortunately, many churches in areas such as the Upper Midwest where I teach remain primarily monocultural. As a result, many young people who aspire to pursue full-time vocational ministry come from these monocultural churches.[2] This limited background influences students' perspectives regarding multicultural ministry. Additionally, many of the pastors and church leaders in these homogeneous communities lack competency when it comes to understanding cultures that differ from their own. If pastors lack cultural competency, this deficit will impact the manner in which they engage (or disengage) diverse populations that exist in their community and virtually every community in America.

Current and future ministers not only need to understand the *importance* of cultural competency, but more importantly, they need to understand how to *increase* their cultural competency. Lamentably, while pastors desire to be more culturally competent, they simply do not know how.

This book provides a pathway to aid present and prospective pastors toward increasing their aptitude related to other cultures. By

---

[1] "New Census Bureau Report Analyzes U.S. Population Projections."

[2] This information was obtained through personal interaction with vocational ministry students in class and on campus.

utilizing this blueprint for increasing one's cultural competency, ministers can be better equipped to minister cross-culturally.

~

This book contains three parts. The first part presents the biblical-theological foundation for the importance of increasing one's cultural competency. The Bible includes a variety of examples regarding cultural competency—some appropriate and some amiss. The chapters in this part focus primarily on examples believers should emulate. However, I explore a few atypical paradigms. The Old Testament (OT) narrates the history of the Jewish people, which records the disdain the Hebrews felt for dissimilar cultures. The biblical account of the Israelites provides equitable cultural competency archetypes. Like the Old Testament, the New Testament (NT) contains contrasting cultural competency annotations. I will explore instances within the life of the Messiah because Jesus serves as the ultimate example of cultural competency. Additionally, I will scrutinize the conflicting actions of the Apostle Peter.

---

As ministers better understand their social environments, increase their cross-cultural effectiveness, and—most importantly—cultivate cultural humility, not only can they better answer the question, "Who is My Neighbor?" but they can *be* the kind of neighbor in their community that God desires.

---

The second part of this book addresses two specific areas. The first focuses on addressing why cultural competency matters. Although one might assume the reason would not need to be argued, the point must be made and the foundation established. Ultimately, the goal of increasing future ministers' cultural competency is at the heart of the section.

Second, I explore the impact of cultural competency in the local church. When ministering cross-culturally, ministers face a variety of barriers that pastors must understand and overcome in order to minister effectively in a cross-cultural context. Ministry leaders today must work not only to understand the nature of racism but to also overcome obstacles in responding in a godly way to it. As ministers better understand their social environments, increase their cross-cultural effectiveness, and—most importantly—cultivate cultural humility, not only can they better answer the question, "Who is My Neighbor?" but they can *be* the kind of neighbor in their community that God desires.

The final part to this book provides practical resources for pastors and church ministry leaders that can be utilized in many ways, such as sermon preparation, leadership training, small group sessions, personal and family devotions, as well as community outreach. The section will engage steps can be leveraged to increase one's cultural competency. However, it is important to recognize that cultural competency is not a final destination, instead it is a continual journey replete with challenges and successes. Despite the potential ups and downs, it is our responsibility to pick up the mantel modeled for us all throughout scripture, ultimately exemplifying a Christ-like life.

# PART ONE

While the twentieth century posed numerous scenarios during which cultural competency was needed, those situations were predicated by an American history that had known slavery as a societal norm. Civil Rights leaders awakened the United States to the disgusting trauma inflicted upon African Americans. The U.S. government took measures to ensure not only freedom for all minorities, but also equality—a dignity so long denied them. Although some people might assume the racial divide in the United States is a unique event in human history, the Bible disproves the notion.

The Old Testament (*Tanakh*[1]) narrates the inception and history of the nation of Israel.[2] Contained within the written account of Jewish history, the reader encounters numerous examples of the enslavement and oppression of the Jews. The reader of Jewish history might not understand that God had designated the Hebrews as an exclusive people group, despite the circumstances in which they often found themselves. The history of God's chosen people provides the modern church with an example of the importance of pursuing cultural competency. The examination of various biblical scenarios provides a platform from which today's church leadership can glean. In so doing, the local church can become a catalyst for change amid the current racial divide in the United States.

---

[1] *Tanakh* is the name for the Hebrew Bible, more widely known as the Torah. *Tanakh* comes from the acronym, TNK for the three main sections of the Hebrew Bible: *Torah* (Pentateuch), *Nevi'im* (Prophets) and *Ketuvim* (Writings). Encyclopedia Britannica, "Hebrew Bible."

[2] This chapter will use various names for the nation of Israel: Israelites, Hebrews, and Jews.

# 1

# *Imago Dei*

At the heart of cultural diversity exists the desire for people, or people groups, to be known or to establish a name. Ironically, to relate identity by means of a name necessarily limits the scope of understanding for a people or people groups. Ultimately, establishing a name seeks to establish identity. Humankind, throughout history, has endeavored to make a name for themselves, while simultaneously seeking to create and cement their identity. Unfortunately, an identity not rooted in God forms a void, which ironically can only be filled by God, creating a cyclical vacuum from which many people never escape. Thus, the quest for a name creates an identity paradox—a bifurcation of sorts. Theological anthropology, which resides at the heart of the Christian concept of the soul, speaks about humankind, as a whole, and the human person, in particular, as a creation of God destined to be the *imago Dei*.[1]

The Christian doctrine of the *imago Dei* is rooted in the Genesis account of creation, specifically the creation of humankind.[2] Although, the theological understanding of *imago Dei* presents various challenges, it is compounded by the Fall.[3] Matthew T. Lee and Amos Yong provide clarity regard what humanity lost at the Fall: "In the Fall divine likeness was lost completely, and the image was corrupted but not completely lost."[4] Therefore, the study of *imago Dei* provides a vital link between identity within society and an identity in God. However, a quandary exists in attempting to align the two identities. Claudia Welz's asserts, "Understanding the *imago dei* as a complex sign that is at once iconic, indexical, and symbolic,—signifying through *deixis* and thereby pointing

---

[1] Grenz, *The Social God and the Relational Self*, 3.

[2] Lee and Yong, *The Science and Theology of Godly Love*, 58.

[3] The Fall references Adam and Eve's sin in the Garden of Eden, creating a separation between God and humankind.

[4] Lee and Yong, *The Science and Theology of Godly Love*, 58.

beyond itself."[5] Welz questions the complexities of *imago Dei*: if humankind was made in God's image, and image is something that is visible, but God is invisible, then how are we made in God's image? Christians must resolve the impasse pointed out by Welz; they must understand that their identity is not rooted in worldly understanding, but rather rooted in identification beyond oneself—God.

---

> Christians must understand that their identity is
> not rooted in worldly understanding, but rather
> in identification beyond oneself—God.

---

To establish a biblical basis for *imago Dei*, one must consult the book of Genesis. *Imago Dei* appears only three times in the *Tanakh* (Gen 1:26-27; 5:1-3; 9:6), but the three Genesis passages are significant. This chapter will address interpretive dilemmas, provide a relevant biblical-theological foundation, establish the framework surrounding *imago Dei*, and discuss the ramifications, not only for the Jews, but also on all of humankind.

Genesis 1:26 serves as the introduction to *imago Dei*, and provides caveats that require examination, thrusting the reader into a greater appreciation of God's intentionality, from the beginning, for diversity. However, to understand the various elements of Genesis 1:26, the reader must start "in the beginning."

## Singular versus Plural

Genesis 1:1-2 introduces God to the reader through his creative power. The name for God in these verses is the Hebrew word אֱלֹהִים, translated as *Elohim*. Although the word for God would seem simple and direct, it has presented itself in a more complex manner—including, not least of all, the Hebrew plural noun that is translated singular to accommodate monotheism. The complication of *Elohim* becomes evident within the second verse of the Bible, when "Genesis 1:2 foreshadows the complexity of *Elohim*."[6]

---

[5] Welz, "Imago Dei," 76.

[6] *Elohim* is the literal translation of אֱלֹהִים, which is the Hebrew word used for God in the Old Testament. Elwell and Beitzel, "Elohim," 697.

Modern readers have the luxury, provided by hindsight, to interpret the mention of *Elohim* (אֱלֹהִים) in Genesis 1:2 as the Holy Spirit. However, without prior knowledge of this interpretation, one might interpret אֱלֹהִים וְרוּחַ as "Spirit of God." Translating אֱלֹהִים וְרוּחַ as "Spirit of God" gives the connotation that the Scripture refers to God's spirit, as opposed to a member of the Trinity. While some people might argue the difference is only semantics, the importance of the differentiation becomes clearer upon reading Genesis 1 where the singular form of *Elohim* (אֱלֹהִים) appears to be the primary thrust until verses 26 and 27. Verse 26 provides "two interpretive dilemmas."[7] First, the verse remains consistent with the prior verses by using אֱלֹהִים, but then causes confusion by switching to נַעֲשֶׂה, which translates as "let us make." The introduction of a plural verb could be dismissed as a translation error if it was an isolated occurrence. However, the plural usage is not an isolated incident, rather, "this is the first of four passages in the Old Testament in which the plural is found in divine dialogue."[8] Verse 26 continues the plural designation by using the noun בְּצַלְמֵנוּ, which translates as "in Our image." To reinforce the plural transition, the verse continues by using the plural again with כִּדְמוּתֵנוּ, which translates "according to Our likeness." While the introduction of three plural statements could produce an interpretative dilemma, these usages serve as the foundation for the theology of *imago Dei*.

Genesis 1:26-27 also shapes an understanding of how the Hebrew preposition *bet*[9] is used in כִּדְמוּתֵנוּ בְּצַלְמֵנוּ. One can see continuity between the Hebrew and the Greek:

> The Septuagint uses the Greek preposition κατά, which implies the same as the English preposition 'in.' God's image is the prototype or example to which the human being is to correspond. This is the traditional Platonic view that can also be found in the Vulgate. This view takes the Hebrew preposition as a *bet normae*. However, if the Hebrew preposition is interpreted as *bet essentiae*, then בְּצַלְמֵנוּ means 'as our image.'[10]

---

[7] Matthews, *Genesis 1-11:26*, 161.

[8] Matthews, *Genesis 1-11:26*, 161.

[9] *Bet* is the second letter in the Hebrew alphabet. "It has been proposed that the letter was originally a crude pictogram of a house. The use of this term as "house" or "dwelling" resulted in its use as a portion of compound place-names such as Bethlehem, Bethel, Bethphage, Bethsaida, and the like." In the context of Genesis 1, *bet* is translated as "in." Powell, "bet, beth," 90.

[10] Welz, "Imago Dei," 76.

Many ancient interpreters concluded that God was indeed addressing some other being or beings, although they did not necessarily agree on whom.[11] The differences in translation may cause confusion, which means it becomes imperative that בְּצַלְמֵנוּ be translated as "in our image." Karl Barth provides a stellar interpretation, reinforcing the need to rectify the interpretive dilemma of plurality. Peter Althouse summarizes Barth:

> God is depicted not as a unified monad but as trinitarian. In other words, the threefold self-differentiation within the One God is taken seriously when grappling with God's image in humanity. What this means is that the divine image from which humanity has been fashioned is an expression of trinitarian relationship that gives to the other in perichoretic fellowship.[12]

Although the differences between "in" and "as" could be argued as mere semantics, the implied meaning between the two words, in conjunction with God's image, could open the door to differing interpretations. Therefore, it is important to understand Barth's point. Barth asserts, "In God's own being and sphere there is a counterpart: a genuine but harmonious self-encounter and self-discovery; a free co-existence and co-operation; an open confrontation and reciprocity. Man is the repetition of this divine life; its copy and reflection."[13] Understanding Genesis 1:26 as humankind being made in God's image, directly ties humanity to God.

The second dilemma encountered in Genesis 1:26 involves the use of the terms image and likeness in relation to humankind. Unfortunately, readers often translate Genesis 1:26 to mean that humanity "looks" like God; to come to such a conclusion represents a misunderstanding of the Scripture, thus creating a false understanding of God. Ascertaining what the likeness to God consists of is quite difficult.[14] Ultimately, "the true image of God is Christ."[15] Humans, in turn, are actually made in Christ's image.[16] The *imago Dei*, then, as an act of God's self-giving character, carries with it the relational quality of self-giving love.[17]

---

11 Kugel, *The Bible as It Was*, 62.

12 Althouse, "Contributions of Christology to the Theology of Godly Love," 60.

13 Barth, *Church Dogmatics*, 185.

14 Keil and Delitzsch, *The Pentateuch*, 39.

15 Grenz, *The Social God and the Relational Self*, 146.

16 Irenaeus, *Proof of the Apostolic Preaching*, 61-63, Kindle.

17 Lee and Yong, *The Science and Theology of Godly Love*, 61.

## Image and Likeness Defined

Scholars have often debated the exact meaning of *imago Dei*. Unfortunately, modern readers attempt to understand the theology of *imago Dei* through a modern interpretive lens. Thus, readers unintentionally commit eisegesis, which further impairs their understanding of *imago Dei*. While the potential for misunderstandings in Scripture exist, one must recognize that "almost any written text contains potential ambiguities."[18] However, the purpose of Christ's incarnation was to bring the fullness of the divine image and likeness to humanity, a fullness that encompasses all dimensions of human existence.[19]

Traditional interpretations of Genesis 1:26 yield two results: *image* or *likeness*. The translated word *image* comes from the Hebrew צֶלֶם. *Image* and *likeness* are probably synonymous terms in Hebrew parallelism.[20]

> The Hebrew word "image" (*selem*) refers to a representation, image, or likeness; it often refers to the way that an idol represented a god. "Likeness" (*demut*) means "similar in appearance," usually visual appearance, but it can also refer to audible similarity. Taken together, "likeness" complements "image" to mean that man is more than a mere image; he is a likeness of God. Yet, regardless of whether one argues from definition or word order, attempts to distinguish sharply "image" from "likeness" are misguided. For centuries theologians have tried to contrast the "image" (as the physical, natural or rational part of man) over and against the "likeness" (as the spiritual, moral, and volitional part of man). While the terms *selem* and *demut* complement one another, three subsequent references to 1:26 all confirm that these two terms are essentially interchangeable ideas in the common Hebrew literary style of parallelism.[21]

By understanding that image or likeness should be understood as a representation presents a different approach when interpreting Genesis 1:26, as well as the other subsequent passages that highlight *imago Dei*. Humankind does not "look" like God, but rather is the representation of God. Cumulative evidence suggests that the biblical *imago Dei* refers to the status or office of the human race as God's authorized stewards, charged

---

<sup></sup>18 Kugel, *The Bible as It Was*, 3.

19 Grenz, *The Social God and the Relational Self*, 146.

20 Manser, *Dictionary of Bible Themes*, Logos.

21 Johnson, "Image of God," 806

with the royal-priestly vocation of representing God's rule on earth through their exercise of cultural power.[22] With this background, a clearer understanding of *imago Dei* begins to emerge. In place of understanding the creation of humankind as a mirror image of God, humankind becomes the depiction of God. Consequently, a cumulative look at Scripture produces an understanding that "calls humans to deepen their relationship with God, relying on divine resources to make deep change possible."[23]

---

> To understand the importance of cultural competency, one must realize that all of humankind serves as the image of God.

---

Additionally, צֶלֶם not only denotes image, but also statue.[24] Egyptian and Assyrian parallels suggest that the pharaoh or king is the living image or manifestation of God during his reign.[25] Here the word for *image* designates a statue that was carried in processions and believed to reveal the deity and exert its power.[26] A statue represented the deity to which it was assigned. It served as a likeness of that particular ruler. Even if an individual had never met the ruler, he or she could still acquire an impression of the person the statue represented. In essence, the statue served to reveal the person it was intended to represent. Therefore, when understanding צֶלֶם as statue, it reinforces the notion that humankind reveals God and, subsequently, his power through the Holy Spirit. The cultural must be understood as intrinsic to what it means to be human, but human as created in the image of God.[27] To understand the importance of cultural competency, one must realize that all of humankind serves as the image of God. The designation is not relegated to a select group, which was the perspective of the Jews; all people are the representation of God.

## The Heart of *Imago Dei*

At the core of *imago Dei* exists the revelation that while humankind represents God, they are also called to know him intimately—an intimacy

---

22 Middleton, *The Liberating Image*, 235.
23 Salvatore E. Farina, "Leadership Development Coaching," 32.
24 Berlejung, *Die Theologie der Bilder*, 308-311.
25 Ockinga, *Die Gottenbenbildlichkeit im Alten Agypten und im Alten Testament*, 153.
26 Welz, "Imago Dei," 76.
27 Medina, *Christianity, Empire and the Spirit*, 354.

unobtainable because of sin. Humanity no longer needs to struggle under the oppressive weight associated with rationalizing that they "look" like God, rather they can embrace the liberty intended by Christ, through the cross and explained by Paul in Romans 8:29.

The plural nature of *imago Dei* provides a framework for understanding diversity. Understanding that humankind was formed in God's image not only helps people identify with God, but also demonstrates that humans were not meant to be alone. Furthermore, when examining the triune God, it quickly becomes apparent that each person of the Godhead demonstrates unique characteristics. The Godhead does not represent three deities who are all the same. Yes, they are divine, but they possess different attributes and even reveal themselves to humankind in different ways. Consequently, to relegate *imago Dei* to only an image strips humanity from understanding the deeper impact of being made in God's image.

As a consequence of the Fall, humankind's image became skewed, but Christ's work on the cross rectifies the misappropriation of humanity's image. To conclude that Jesus's death (and resurrection) served only as an offering for sin limits the redemptive work of the cross, as noted in the *Holman Illustrated Bible Dictionary*:

> The biblical picture of imago Dei means that all human beings, not just kings, possess special royal status as God's appointed stewards over the earth. By virtue of mankind's ruling over the rest of God's creatures and earth, every member of the human race somehow represents and reflects the sovereign Lord of creation.[28]

Understanding *imago Dei* as image and statue, based on the previous explanation, provides an appropriate context for interpreting the creation of Adam and Eve as the image, or representation, of God.

## Adam and Eve and Their Descendants

"In the beginning," the first three words of the Torah, provide a framework for biblical theology, because biblical theology must start in the beginning. Consequently, to establish a solid biblical theology for understanding cultural competency, this section will examine foundational

---

[28] Johnson, "Image of God," 807.

examples of diversity, in addition to other elements of cultural competency paramount to the topic.

The Genesis creation account records God's acts of creating the known world, including the creation of man. Within this account of the creation of man, one should examine several important details. First, the Hebrew word for "man" or "humankind" is אָדָם. Unfortunately, the usage of אָדָם fosters ambiguity when interpreting the text. When Genesis 1:27 states that God "created man," it utilizes אָדָם. The usage of אָדָם remains consistent until Genesis 2:20, where the Hebrew word is the same but instead of translating it as "man," the Bible translation ascribes the designation of "Adam"; אָדָם appears twice before another designation is made. Keep in mind that the Old Testament Hebrew had no common term for "humanity" other than *adam*.[29]

Whether אָדָם translates as "Adam" or "man," the key element is to note the intentionality in establishing a link—not only between God and Adam but also between God and humankind. While God is linked to the whole of humanity, he is also linked to man individually through Adam. Had the Scriptures referenced אָדָם only in the broader sense of humankind, intimacy would have been lost. Instead, God sought to establish a deeper connection. Although God has created people as individuals, embedded in the nature of *imago Dei* is the tension of being autonomous people who dwell in disparate communities.[30] God was not content to simply rule all of humankind; he desired personal relationship with individuals.

One primary reason to establish the presence of the man Adam within the Genesis account, as opposed to the humankind debate created by the dual usage of אָדָם, is that Genesis 5 provides the genealogy of Adam. One must reference the New Testament to fully understand its impact. The first genealogy of the Bible begins, and the last genealogy in the Bible ends, not with any human individual but with God.[31] Therefore, Adam's genealogy becomes pivotal because it provides a direct connection to Jesus Christ.

The relation between Adam and Jesus Christ becomes foundational for understanding *imago Dei*. Theological accounts of the *imago Dei* tend to draw from Genesis 1:26-28 rather than Genesis 5:1-3.[32] The Genesis 5 omission can even be seen in the writings of well-known

---

29 Hess, "Equality with and without Innocence," 80.
30 Westbrook, "New Reflections on Mirror Neuron Research," 322-337.
31 Ortlund, "Image of Adam, Son of God," 673-688.
32 Ortlund, "Image of Adam, Son of God," 673-688.

theologians such as Millard Erickson, whose discourse concerning *imago Dei* simply skips from Genesis 1 to Genesis 9.[33] The lengthy accounts of the *imago Dei* in Augustine, Aquinas, and Calvin have repeated interaction with Genesis 1, but never with Genesis 5.[34]

Origen, however, sought to make the *imago Dei* connection utilizing Genesis 5 by addressing a connection with the *Imago Adami*. Origen surmises, "Christ is the invisible image of the invisible God, in the same manner as we say, according to the sacred history, that the image of Adam is his son Seth."[35] Origen then makes the argument that "this image contains the unity of nature and substance belonging to the Father and the Son."[36] Walter Brueggemann calls the *Imago Adami* "an odd ambiguous statement."[37] As a result, Brueggemann's assessment points to why many commentators seem to dismiss the *imago Dei* connection in Genesis 5, which may be the wrong conclusion.

When commentators have brought Genesis 5:3 into the discussion concerning *imago Dei*, the tendency has been to reduce its significance to the extension of the image to Adam's descendants.[38] However, such a conclusion would be a travesty. One must follow the connection of *imago Dei* from Genesis 1 to Genesis 5. In so doing, one can connect Genesis 5 with Luke 3:38, which leads to the conclusion that "the *imago Dei* is not obliterated by the fall, but continues to Adam's posterity."[39] God's image was, therefore, not peculiar to the first man but inherited in successive generations.[40] The image of God passes through Adam; thus, a parallel is drawn between God creating and Adam procreating.[41]

---

[33] Erickson, *Christian Theology*, 519.

[34] Works consulted for this conclusion include Augustine, *The Fathers of the Church*, 45-141; Aquinas, *Summa Theologica*, 469-477; and Calvin, *Institutes of the Christian Religion*, 183-196.

[35] Origen, *De Principiis*, 247-248.

[36] Origen, *De Principiis*, 247-248.

[37] Brueggemann, *Genesis*, 68.

[38] Ortlund, "Image of Adam, Son of God," 676.

[39] Ortlund, "Image of Adam, Son of God," 676.

[40] von Rad, *Genesis: A Commentary*, 70.

[41] Ortlund, "Image of Adam, Son of God," 678.

# 2

# A Biblical History of Diversity

The image and likeness of God is found in human differentiation, specifically the differentiation of male and female.[1] Karl Barth's use of "man" should be understood as the whole of humanity, not as individual:

> The only thing that we are told about the creation of man, apart from the fact that it was accomplished by the Word of God in and after the image of God, is that "God created them male and female." … The only real differentiation and relationship is that of man to man, and in its original and most concrete form of man to woman and woman to man. Man is no more solitary than God. But as God is one, and He alone is God, so man is one and alone, and two only in the duality of his kind, i.e., the duality of man and woman.[2]

The importance of the biblical distinction between male and female, coupled with God's revelation regarding his triune nature, provides the theological framework for understanding God and man, while also establishing the distinct nature of each entity. Therefore, when the biblical author utilizes אָדָם, in conjunction with the creation of Eve, it presents an even more diverse nature to God and humankind.

The accounts of creation, the Garden of Eden, and the Fall in Genesis 1-3 may contain more doctrinal teaching concerning the nature of humanity as male and female and the state of the fallen world than any other single text in the Bible. Their position at the beginning of the Torah, and thus of Scripture as a whole, makes them an important starting point for the study of the biblical teaching on gender equality.[3] Through Eve, the biblical reader begins to interpret the evolving definition of *imago Dei*. It is highly important to understand that not only does Adam represent *imago Dei*, but that Eve does as well. *Imago Dei* passes not only from Adam but also from Eve to their firstborn child, Seth, thereby solidifying the theological connection made in Genesis 1, Genesis 5, and Adam's lineage.

---

[1] Lee and Yong, *The Science and Theology of Godly Love*, 61.

[2] Barth, *Church Dogmatics*, 185-186.

[3] Hess, "Equality with and without Innocence," 81.

Although one can conclude that *imago Dei* was intact despite the Fall, sin has skewed humanity's ability to understand their identity in light of *imago Dei*. To understand the confusion facing humanity's identity framework, the Genesis story takes an intriguing turn.

## Diversity at the Tower of Babel

Genesis 11 documents the history of the Tower of Babel, a story illustrating humankind's desire for a collective name, a desire for identity, a desire to pursue their own endeavors. Within the historical account of the Tower of Babel exists an intriguing biblical introduction to the cultural bifurcation present in the world. The narrative of Babel explains the origin of multiple languages in the world, which would ultimately lead to new cultures. As a result, the disbursement at Babel presents itself as the starting point for a broader understanding of cultural diversity.

---

The disbursement at Babel presents itself as the starting point for a broader understanding of cultural diversity.

---

Following the great Flood, as documented in Genesis 6-9, a group of people desired universal identity, and they endeavored to build a city. Within the new municipality, the people wanted to build "a tower whose top will reach into heaven" (Gen 11:4b). Unfortunately, God did not look favorably upon their quest. The task of building a tower was not inherently evil; after all, what was wrong about what the builders had tried to do?[4] The answer lies in the stated resolve. While one might surmise their only purpose was to build a tower to heaven, an ulterior motive was obvious only to God. To fully understand the infraction, one must look back in Genesis at God's command prior to the Babel account.

Genesis 1:29 records God saying, "Be fruitful and multiply, and fill the earth." From the beginning of creation, God gave the mandate for humankind to fill the earth. Moving forward, it can be assumed that people multiplied and spread. However, the spreading of humankind is disrupted during the time of Noah. Because of the rampant sin and godlessness, God destroys everything with the Flood, except for Noah and his family.

---

[4] Kugel, *The Bible as It Was*, 123.

When Noah disembarks from the Ark, God again repeats the mandate given in Genesis 1. God blesses Noah and his sons and says to them, "Be fruitful and multiply, and fill the earth" (Gen 9:1). Again, in verse 7, God states, "As for you, be fruitful and multiply; populate the earth abundantly and multiply in it." Twice, at critical junctures in human history, God gives the command to multiply and spread. Chapter 10 of Genesis records the multiplying and spreading of Noah's descendants—the fulfillment of God's command.

The proliferation of humanity appears to commence soon after the Flood. Genesis 10 documents the genealogies of Noah's descendants. However, at some point in the process, humankind deviates from God's commission to multiply and fill the earth, which brings the focus back to the Tower of Babel. Not only did the people want to establish identity by making a name for themselves, but they also justified their reason with the rationale: "Otherwise we will be scattered abroad over the face of the whole earth" (Gen 11:4). The tower hides the true intent of man's actions—a choice not to obey God's mandate. David I. Smith and Barbara Carvill reveal the outcome: "God intervenes in a way that not only judges and disrupts the empire-building project, but also pushes the builders back onto the path God had originally set before them."[5] While some people may interpret God's actions as vindictive or punitive, perhaps God's mediation introduces a redemptive element.

Ultimately, humankind's existence as a monolinguistic culture changed. Prior to Babel, people groups were determined by geographic location. After Babel, geographic location and language defined a person's identity and, subsequently, their family, tribe, and culture. Consequently, the story of the Tower of Babel presents unique dynamics that specifically address the origin of cultural diversity. Adi Shmueli notes, that the root of the story is the quest for a name at any cost, even if it means conflicting with God's plan:

> A human being draws his identity from a group. You are what you are partly because you belong to this or that group of people. You speak their language, behave as they taught you to behave. You are French, English or a New Yorker with a Bronx accent. In each case your identity is deter-mined in a social context. And it is this

---

[5] Smith and Carvill, *The Gift of the Stranger*, 8.

identity that the people of Babel sought in trying to find themselves a name.[6]

While the outcome of the story of Babel has a negative connotation, perhaps God had a different plan. The Babel story should not be read pessimistically; rather it should be understood as the continuation of God's plan. Néstor Medina asserts, "Diversity is part of the divine creation, part of the work of God."[7] Medina's conclusion lends credibility to recognizing Babel, not as a scattering, but as a fulfillment of God's design. Timothy Paul Westbrook also sees the text in a positive light: "[It] turns the focus away from punishment and views the Tower of Babel narrative as primarily being an origination story of cultural heterogeneity."[8] Westbrook views "multiple languages not as a curse or punishment, instead, it rather firmly places the narrative in the context of Genesis 1-11, as God demonstrates his intention to create a plurality of human experiences."[9] Multiple languages cause a disbursement to occur, spreading humanity and dividing them not only by geographical location but also by different dialects. Seeing plurality of culture and ethnicity as part of God's plan for creation aligns with images and doctrines in the New Testament that seek to join Jews and Gentiles into one people of God while maintaining cultural identities for the glory of God.[10]

---

Medina's conclusion lends credibility to recognizing Babel, not as a scattering, but as a fulfillment of God's design.

---

In a reading of the first eleven chapters of Genesis, events may seem incoherent. At times, Scripture records what could be deemed as expressions of God's emotions, many of which also seem random. The Genesis creation account expresses God's delight with his creation. However, Genesis 1:31 records that on the sixth day God saw what he had created and deviated from his typical feeling of good (טוֹב) and instead expresses his delight by adding the adjective very (מְאֹד). God felt differently

---

[6] Shmueli, *The Tower of Babel: Identity and Sanity*, 2.
[7] Medina, *Christianity, Empire and the Spirit*, 353.
[8] Westbrook, "New Reflections," 323.
[9] Westbrook, "New Reflections," 324.
[10] Westbrook, "New Reflections," 327.

about his creation on the sixth day than he did on the other days. God's expressions can also be seen in the creation of Eve. God demonstrated empathy by recognizing, "It is not good for the man to be alone; I will make him a helper suitable for him" (Gen 2:18). Genesis 6:6 records God experiencing regret and pain: "The Lord was sorry that he had made man on the earth, and he was grieved in his heart." As a result of humanity's transgression, God brought about the great Flood. With the receding of the floodwaters and Noah's burnt offering, God's anger is soothed (הַנִּיחֹחַ) (Gen 8:21). As a result, God declares that he will never destroy every living thing again.

Although the events in themselves may seem random or chaotic, they demonstrate God's redemptive desire and culminate with the Babel story. Genesis 11:5 seems to connote that God was surprised by human actions, and he decided to act. In the Babel story, twice the author highlights the fact that people are once again spreading out over the earth, suggesting that a more final judgement is being averted and humankind is being returned to a path with the possibility of blessing.[11]

---

> Diversity becomes a tool that God uses
> to achieve His goals.

---

Instead of viewing God's response as random and reactive, readers must understand His actions in terms of His desire to avert judgment, thus allowing His people to pursue a future blessing found only when people follow God's commands. The Babel story introduces diverse languages as a means to accomplish God's edict to be fruitful and multiply. The scattering of the people must be understood as an unmitigated good because it forced humanity-now diversified, to fulfill God's creational commission.[12] Therefore, diversity becomes a tool that God uses to achieve his goals.

## The Diversity of Israel

According to the book of Acts, even the Apostle Peter demonstrated a lack of desire to present the gospel to Gentiles (Acts 10). His objection centered on an aversion to increasing his cultural

---

11 Smith and Carvill, *The Gift of the Stranger*, 8.
12 Medina, *Christianity, Empire and the Spirit*, 349.

competency. To fully understand the exchange between Peter and Cornelius, the reader must understand the history of Israel, specifically related to the mandate not to intermingle with other cultures.

---

## Peter's objection centered on an aversion to increasing his cultural competency.

---

Exodus 12 recounts the narrative of the Passover, which presents a redemptive illustration of the blood of lambs providing protection from death. After the first Passover, the captive Israelites are commanded to leave Egypt. Exodus 12:38 indicates that the Israelites were not the only ones to leave Egypt: "A mixed multitude also went up with them." This presents an interesting paradigm for understanding the Jewish people as well as for understanding diversity.

The Hebrew word עֵרֶב translates as "mixture, mixed company."[13] The straightforward translation of עֵרֶב does not present ambiguity but rather confirms that fact that the Israelites of the exodus (and thereafter) were actually an ethnically mixed people—something most Christians do not know.[14] H. D. M. Spence-Jones provides some insight into who comprised this mixed company:

> Kalisch supposes that these strangers were native Egypt-ians, anxious to escape the tyranny of the kings. Canon Cook suggests that they were "remains of the old Semitic population" of the Eastern provinces. Perhaps it is more probable that they consisted of fugitives from other subject races (as the Shartana) oppressed by the Pharaohs.[15]

The importance of clarifying the diversity of the group of Israelites provides a foundation for understanding cultural diversity, especially in light of the various ethnic tensions Israel would face in the future.

Some scholars have argued that the reference to a "mixed company" only referred to a small group; fortunately, Moses[16] quickly dispatched a numerical designation for עֵרֶב. According to Exodus 12:38,

---


[13] Thomas, *New American Standard Dictionaries*, Logos.

[14] Stuart, *Exodus*, 297.

[15] Spence-Jones, *Exodus*, 288.

[16] This assumes that Moses authored the book of Exodus.

Moses states that the "mixed company" was actually a "multitude" (רַב).[17] A multitude can only be understood as a large group. The *Holman Illustrated Bible Dictionary* clarifies that the "mixed multitude" of Exodus was not a single occurrence. While the term "mixed multitude" is used in the Exodus account, it also appears in other places. Brand indicates that "the term is used for those foreigners who joined with the Israelites in the exodus from Egypt (Exod 12:38), who became associated with the people of Judah during the exile (Neh 13:3), or who were associated with the Egyptians (Jer 25:20) or Babylonians (Jer 50:37)."[18] Interestingly, the mixed multitude of Israel was not an anomaly found in the Exodus account. Although, it began in Egypt, occurrences continue throughout the Old Testament, and seem to culminate near the end of the Jewish historical record provided by Nehemiah. Throughout the Torah, numerous references point to a person who is not considered an Israelite. The Old Testament text utilizes the following designations for the non-Israelite: foreigner, alien, sojourner, and stranger.

## The Diversity of the Foreigner

The Exodus account introduces the term *foreigner*, which is used interchangeably with "noncitizen or alien, temporary guest, sojourner, or stranger."[19] In the Hebrew language, the word appears in various forms. Exodus 2, 20, 22, and 23 uses the term גֵּר, which translates as "a sojourner."[20] However, in Exodus 12:43, Moses deviates from the Hebrew word "גֵּר" and utilizes "נֵכָר" instead; נֵכָר translates literally as "a foreigner."[21] The introduction of the term *foreigner* reinforces a clear designation between the Israelites and those who were not Hebrews.

The foreigner designation provides an important distinction in Scripture. The people who carry the designation of foreigner are not included with the ambiguous אָדָם, (usually translated as "[hu]mankind") but rather indicates separate people groups. While the difference between Israelites and foreigners seems simple, the importance lies with understanding that the Hebrews were not a "pure" race. Additionally, the *foreigner* moniker reinforces the need for a biblical theology of cultural diversity, and an understanding of cultural competency. In addition to גֵּר

---

17 Thomas, *New American Standard Dictionaries*, Logos.
18 Brand, "Mixed Multitude," 1145.
19 Elwell and Beitzel, "Foreigner," 806.
20 Thomas, *New American Standard Dictionaries*, Logos.
21 Thomas, *New American Standard Dictionaries*, Logos.

being translated as "foreigner," the word translates as "alien," "stranger," or "sojourner."[22] The word appears in the Torah eighty-three times, and in each instance one of the previously mentioned words is utilized. Ultimately, the גֵּר, particularly from the perspective of the Jew, referred to the immigrants, the temporary or permanent residents who have come from abroad, possibly to find shelter from exclusion or conflict.[23]

The Law of Moses outlines the way the Israelites were to treat the foreigners. Ironically, as Smith and Carvill notes, the various regulations in the Pentateuch aimed to prevent Israel from treating the sojourners as the children of Israel had been treated in Egypt:

> The laws concerning the stranger appeal to the Israelites' own experience, urging them to treat as they themselves wish others had treated them. Of course, this does not mean they are to relinquish the integrity of their identity and cultural home, or to romantically accept all things foreign, as the ongoing polemic against destructive idolatry makes clear (e.g., Exod. 34:15-17). Rather, the alien is to respect the same community standards and laws as the Israelite (e.g., Exod. 12:49). Welcoming the alien does not put Israel's faith and communal ways up for sale; it is precisely that faith and God's expectations of the community that are to motivate a loving welcome for the stranger. Israel's faith is not to be sacrificed to hospitality; instead, it undergirds it. Welcoming the stranger does not involve an abandonment of identity for Israel. Rather, it involves the formation of an identity expressed in love.[24]

Essentially, the Israelites were encouraged not to repeat the atrocities imposed on them; instead, God commanded them, "show your love for the alien, for you were aliens in the land of Egypt" (Deut 10:19). More specifically, God dictates to the Israelites, "When a stranger resides with you in your land, you shall not do him wrong. The stranger who resides with you shall be to you as the native among you, and you shall love him as yourself, for you were aliens in the land of Egypt; I AM the Lord your God" (Lev 19:33-34). God's command continues to echo today. We must seek to love others as we love ourselves.

---

22 Thomas, *New American Standard Dictionaries,* Logos.
23 Meyers and O'Connor, *The Word of the Lord Shall Go Forth,* 321.
24 Smith and Carvill, *The Gift of the Stranger,* 11.

# 3

# Biblical Examples of Cultural Competency

Throughout the remainder of the Old Testament, the emphasis is primarily on the history of Israel. The notion of foreigners or sojourners does not represent much of the historical narrative—at least until the post-exilic period of Ezra and Nehemiah. The concluding chapter of Nehemiah presents an interesting narrative regarding ethnic diversity. Following the dedication of the wall, Nehemiah reads to the people from the Scriptures. Mervin Breneman makes the following observation: "There is no indication that this was a special occasion. Rather it was the regular liturgical reading from Scripture, the source of encouragement and the standard of behavior of every healthy community of God's people."[1] While it was standard practice for a leader to read Scripture to the people, Nehemiah chooses an interesting passage: Deuteronomy 23. To understand the implication of the passage Nehemiah read, understanding the setting and authorship of Nehemiah 12 and 13 proves helpful.

H. G. M. Williamson indicates the uniqueness of the writing of Nehemiah: "It has long been recognized—and is today universally agreed—that substantial parts of the Book of Nehemiah go back to a first-person account by Nehemiah himself. The conventional term 'Nehemiah Memoir' is retained here for convenience."[2] Nehemiah 12 and 13 appear to be portions taken from Nehemiah's memoir. However, scholars surmise that Nehemiah 12:44 through Nehemiah 13:3 did not originate from Nehemiah's memoir; the writer of these Scriptures inserted into Nehemiah's memoir remains a mystery.[3] The significance of the authorship of the above-mentioned verses points to the need of the writer to ensure future readers knew that Amorites and Moabites were not allowed to enter the assembly of God. Due to this clarification, the reader could conclude that, up till this point, Amorites and Moabites may have been able to enter the assembly of God, which is validated by the covenant in Nehemiah 9 and 10.

---

[1] Breneman, *Ezra, Nehemiah, Esther*, 268.

[2] Williamson, *Ezra, Nehemiah*, xxiv.

[3] Breneman and Williamson both allude indirectly to the mystery writer, although neither person provides clarity regarding who wrote the sections in question.

The declaration of the covenant is revealed at the end of Nehemiah 9 followed by the names that appeared on the covenant (Neh 10). Nehemiah 10:28-30 declares a separation from the people of the land. In addition, the determination to marry outside their kinsmen is abolished. Nehemiah's edict regarding marrying foreigners coincides with Ezra 9:1-2, which outlines Ezra's disdain to the revelation that the Israelites have married foreigners. Nehemiah's proclamation in chapter 13 appears to advocate for segregation. As a result of the Scripture that Nehemiah reads, the people conclude: "So when they heard the law, they excluded foreigners from Israel" (Neh 13:3). Although Breneman asserts, "Removal of foreigners should not be viewed as racial exclusivism,"[4] the spirit behind the edict elicits an exclusivist ideology. Consequently, despite the oppression that the Jews had experienced and despite God's warnings not to repeat the offenses perpetrated on them, they still attempted to separate themselves from those of non-Jewish descent.

Despite the prevalent Jewish mindset that foreigners or Gentiles should not be viewed as equal with the Hebrews, there are examples of individuals who broke cultural norms and attempted to bridge the gap between Jews and Gentiles. Interestingly, Joseph, Moses, and Ruth played significant roles in Jewish history and provide a framework for understanding the importance of increased cultural competency and the subsequent blessing that ensues. The following sections address their stories.

## Joseph (Genesis 37:1-36)

The story of Joseph serves as an example of the tension that exists among various cultural groups and the reconciliation necessary to move toward cultural competence. Genesis 37 establishes an intriguing dichotomy because it labels Jacob, the patriarch of Israel, as a sojourner or foreigner. The father of the nation of Israel establishes his descendants' inception as foreigners. Furthermore, the land the Israelites would eventually inhabit was not their original land. Prior to the establishment of the Israelites in the new land to which God had called them, the book of Genesis records the lives of three men known as the patriarchs of the nation of Israel: Abraham, Isaac, and Jacob.[5] All three men were

---

[4] Breneman, *Ezra, Nehemiah, Esther,* 268.
[5] Jacob's name would later be changed to Israel.

sojourners in another land. As a result, Joseph (the son of Jacob) serves as one of the first biblical examples of cultural competency.

---

## Joseph serves as one of the first biblical examples of cultural competency.

---

Joseph's father, grandfather, and great grandfather were sojourners or foreigners. The Bible repeatedly asserts that the patriarchs were a nomadic people.[6] While their nomadic status does not necessarily equate with cultural competency, it demonstrates that the nation of Israel could assimilate into other cultures to survive. Ultimately, the skills of assimilating and understanding are at the core of becoming culturally competent.

The events in the life of Joseph after he was sold into slavery take an ironic twist when he was sold to Ishmaelites who then sold him to the Egyptians. While in Egypt, he eventually served in Pharaoh's court and as second-in-command over all the land. During his reign, Joseph took an Egyptian wife, which means his children would have been half Hebrew and half Egyptian. Additionally, biblical evidence exists to indicate that Joseph successfully assimilated into Egyptian culture. For instance, when Joseph's brothers come to Egypt to buy grain, Scripture indicates that Joseph uses an interpreter, thereby implying that he spoke Egyptian to his brothers and someone else interpreted for him (Gen 42:23). Also, when Joseph and his family take his father's body to be buried in Canaan, the Canaanites think the group is Egyptian (50:11). Although Scripture does not account for the Canaanites' assumption, it can be surmised, based on the appearance and actions of Joseph's group, that they had successfully assimilated into Egyptian culture. Ultimately, Joseph's experiences demonstrate that to become culturally competent one must understand what it is like to live in Egypt.

---

6 Genesis 12 begins with God commanding Abraham to leave his country and become a nomad. Genesis 18:1 depicts Abraham sitting at the door of his tent, again, a reference to nomadic life. Genesis 23-27 show Abraham, Isaac, and Jacob continuing to live in tents. It was not until Joseph was sold into slavery, and his brothers came to settle in Egypt (Gen 47), that they ceased their transient way of life.

## Moses (Exodus 2:1-15)

Exodus, the second book of the Pentateuch, transitions from the lives of the patriarchs to Moses, the man God would use to lead the Israelites out of captivity and into the Promised Land. While not considered one of the patriarchs, Moses retains a lofty status throughout Scripture. Moses arrives on the scene during a period of great oppression in Jewish history.

The series of events in Moses's life are important for building a framework for recognizing him as an example of cultural competency. Moses was born a Hebrew, but he was raised and educated as an Egyptian (Acts 7:22) However, Scripture clearly indicates that Moses had awareness regarding his ethnicity (Exod 2:11). Moses demonstrates cultural competency by maintaining an understanding of his own cultural identity, while also embracing Egyptian culture. Moses grasped Egyptian culture to such an extent that when he fled to Midian, he was reported as being an Egyptian (v. 19).

When Moses returned to Egypt to ask for the release of the Israelites, he expresses an understanding of Egyptian religious practices (Exod 8:26). Moses understood that the animal sacrifices of the Israelites would be abominable to the Egyptians, who were pantheists.[7] D. K. Stuart indicates that the Egyptians opposed animal sacrifice because "they detested anything related to mountain-dwelling peoples' habits and preferences, including the raising of sheep and goats."[8] Moses illustrates cultural competency through these actions.

## Ruth (Ruth 1-4)

The story of Ruth presents an intriguing historical narrative, which provides a framework for establishing a theology of cultural competency. Ruth is important in Jewish history primarily because she appears in David's lineage (Ruth 4:13-22). For Christians, Ruth is important because she appears in Jesus's lineage (Matt 1:5). While Ruth's connection to King David and Jesus is pivotal, it is also controversial because she was not a Jew, but rather a Moabite (Ruth 1:4).

At the inception of the book of Ruth, the author mentions many different locations and cultural groups. The record goes to great length to document that Ruth does not belong ethnically. The tension between the

---

[7] Stuart, *Exodus*, 218.
[8] Stuart, *Exodus*, 218.

Israelites and Moabites is recorded in Genesis 19:30-38. In essence, the Moabites came into existence due to the incestuous relationship of Lot and his oldest daughter. Therefore, the Israelites viewed the Moabites as an incestuous people. The child of the incestuous relationship of Lot and his younger daughter produced the Ammonites. Deuteronomy 23:3 states, "No Ammonite or Moabite shall enter the assembly of the Lord; none of their descendants, even to the tenth generation, shall enter the assembly of the Lord." Interestingly, Moses explains the logic behind the exclusion of Moabites, but the reasoning is not incest. Moses emphasizes the failure of the Moabites to help the Israelites as they left Egypt (Deut 23:3-4) and the mishap with Balaam (Num 22:22-34). As a result, the Moabites were prohibited from entering the assembly of the Lord.

Since Moabites were forbidden from temple worship, the presence of Ruth in the Torah could be viewed as scandalous. Nevertheless, "Ruth's place in the canon was never seriously questioned."[9] Additionally, "The book of Ruth does not hide the fact that Ruth was not a Jew. Of twelve occurrences of the name 'Ruth' in the book, 'the Moabitess' is added five times as a reminder that she was an alien."[10] Therefore, the mixed multitude narrative, as outlined in a previous section, is perpetuated through Ruth.

---

## Ruth the Moabitess demonstrates cultural competency by embracing Jewish culture.

---

Not only does the book of Ruth present rich context for understanding cultural competency, but it also presents a reprieve in Jewish history, as noted by Eugene F. Roop:

> Most biblical stories from the days when the judges ruled tell of life far more violent and dangerous (Ruth 1:1). We read of deadly conflict between Deborah and the Canaanite prince Sisera (Judg 4-5), the exploits of Samson among the Philistines (Judg 14-16), and the raging revenge of the Levite against Gibeah (Judg 19-21). Thus the violence in the stories of Judges only serves to highlight the relative serenity of life in Bethlehem.[11]

---

[9] Gaebelein and Polcyn, *Deuteronomy - 2 Samuel*, 513.

[10] Gaebelein and Polcyn, *Deuteronomy - 2 Samuel*, 527.

[11] Roop, *Ruth, Jonah, Esther: Believers Church Bible Commentary*, EBSCOhost.

Despite the many cultural barriers facing Ruth the Moabitess, she demonstrates cultural competency by embracing Jewish culture.[12] The consequences of her cultural awareness solidify her status as a key figure within the lineage of the Messiah.

[12] Aflred Edersheim outlines the ways in which Ruth demonstrated knowledge of Jewish culture, in addition to embracing Jewish culture (Ruth 1:16-17; 2:2-3; 2:10-14; 3:9). Edersheim, *The Bible History, Old Testament*, 390-399.

# 4

# The New Testament Cultural Shift

The meaning for the term *foreigner* shifts during the transition from the Old Testament to the New Testament. In the Old Testament, foreigner carries a negative connotation, denoting a person who does not belong, but in the New Testament the Greek word προσήλυτος (foreigner) provides a different perspective. The shift provides important context regarding the mind-set necessary to develop a healthy understanding of cultural competency.

In the New Testament, the Greek word for "proselyte" (προσήλυτος, foreigner) generally refers to a stranger in sympathy with Judaism (Matt 23:15; Acts 2:10; 6:5); it can also mean a convert to Christianity.[1] Like the Old Testament, the New Testament utilizes a variety of words to communicate the idea of a foreigner. Often, the designation of "foreigner" was given to Samaritans and Canaanites. While the traditional Jew would have viewed the Samaritans and Canaanites as outsiders, the Apostle Paul presents a different perspective by explaining the theological shift that occurred as a result of Jesus.

At the time of Jesus, the Jewish nation was resolved to live under oppression until the Messiah emerges. Roman rule further ingrained the notion that they should not accept outsiders, foreigners, or their oppressors, also known as Gentiles—essentially anyone who was not Jewish. As a result, the differentiation between Jew and Gentile further propelled the Jews into an exclusive approach to God. The Hebrews viewed themselves as religiously superior (Deut 7:6), which caused them to contradict the commands given to them in the Law of Moses regarding welcoming the stranger (Lev 19:8).[2]

Jesus confronted the Jewish misconception by referencing Gentile groups, even going so far as to mention Samaritans.[3] Consequently, Jesus provides the perfect illustration of cultural competence. He demonstrated

---

[1] Songer, "Proselytes," 1336.

[2] Leviticus 19 lists many ways that an Israelite should treat others, but specifically, Leviticus 19:18 serves as the basis for Jesus's comment in Mark 12:31, "You shall love your neighbor as yourself." For an Israelite to not love and care for his or her neighbor was a violation of Mosaic Law.

[3] The Jewish disdain for Samaritans will be addressed later in the chapter.

inclusion, sensitivity, cultural understanding, religious mastery, and he did not shy away from addressing said topics. Jesus confronted the tension between Jew and Gentile and provided his listeners with a different perspective.

---

> Jesus provides the perfect illustration of cultural competence. He demonstrated inclusion, sensitivity, cultural understanding, and religious mastery.

---

The advent of Jesus Christ transformed human history. Not only did the birth of the Messiah threaten political structures, but it also affected obsolete and static religious structures. The religious elite of the day had extensive control over the Jewish people. Unfortunately, modern Western readers have difficulty comprehending the inter-twined nature of Jewish life and religion; therefore, they struggle to understand the tension under which the Hebrews lived.

Today, American culture understands religion through the lens of "separation of Church and State." Consequently, to the modern or postmodern American, the idea of a society in which the secular and the religious are synonymous and undistinguished is peculiar and unfamiliar. In the time of Jesus, anyone born a Jew would practice Judaism; to deny one's practice of Judaism would equate to denying one's cultural heritage.

## Jesus as the Ultimate Example of Cultural Competency

Jesus is the perfect example of what it means to be culturally competent. Not only did he understand the various nuances of the Jewish leaders of his day (Pharisaic, Sadducean, and Essene), but he also understood the world of the Gentiles.[4] While ethnic boundaries restricted Jewish interaction with Gentiles, Jesus often stepped over the cultural barriers and engaged ostracized individuals or people the Jews viewed as unclean and unworthy.

To understand Jesus as the ultimate example of cultural competency, one must examine the instructions that Jesus imparts to Peter

---

[4] *Gentile* is a term used to describe non-Jews.

in John 21:1517, and then to all the disciples in Acts 1:6-8. However, to comprehend the importance of Jesus's charge, one must first see his interaction with the Samaritans and the woman at the well (John 4) because it establishes the direction of the first-century Church.

## The Samaritans

The Samaritans lived in the area to the north of Judea, but not as far north as Galilee. While determining the physical location of the Samaritans does not pose an issue, their origins do present some difficulties. Based on various historical records and consultation of several biblical experts, consensus persists that "it is difficult to determine precisely when the Samaritan sect arose and when the final break with Judaism occurred."[5] The Samaritans were "mixed inhabitants"[6] who were physically imported from Babylon and other places. These mixed inhabitants were forced to resettle in the cities of Samaria. Over time, the new inhabitants "amalgamated with the Jews still remaining in the land, and gradually abandoned their old idolatry and adopted partly the Jewish religion."[7] Despite the Samaritans' eventual acceptance of Judaism, traditional Jews of Jesus's day viewed the mixed inhabitants with disdain.[8]

The post-exilic period presented several challenges for the Jews. One struggle came directly from the Samaritans:

> The ancient tension between the northern and southern kingdoms was revived with the return of exiles to Jerusalem under Persian ruler Cyrus' edict. The entire southern area was being governed from Samaria in the north by Sanballat, a native ruler of Palestine under Persian authority. The return of exiles to Jerusalem, particularly with their intentions of rebuilding the Jerusalem temple, posed an obvious political threat to his leadership in the north.[9]

The Book of Nehemiah confirms Sanballat's perceived political threat from the Jews (Neh. 2:10, 19; 4:1, 7; 6:1-14). No wonder Ezra eventually felt the need to expel Gentiles during the reconstruction of the temple.

---

5 Elwell and Beitzel, "Samaritans," 1886-1888; additional sources consulted: Potts, "Samaria, Samaritans," 1435-1437. See also Ewing, "Samaritans," 2673-2674.

6 Easton, "Samaritans," Logos.

7 Easton, "Samaritans," Logos.

8 Elwell, Potts, and Ewing all document the views Jews had toward Samaritans.

9 Elwell and Beitzel, "Samaritans," 1887.

Modern readers can only speculate as to Ezra's motive regarding the expulsion of the Gentiles, but it may have been justifiable considering the political tension. Regardless, tensions would continue to mount between the two groups for the next 400 years.[10]

As a result of being shunned by the Jews, the Samaritans proceeded to erect their own temple on Mount Gerizim. Josephus, the renowned historian, recounts the events surrounding the Samaritan temple conflict by noting that, around 130 to 120 BC, a Jewish Hasmonean king destroyed the temple and the whole city.[11] As a result of the destruction, tensions between the two groups reached a climax.

Following the destruction of the Samaritan temple, the inhabitants of Samaria erected a second temple located at Shechem. Amid the strain between Samaritans and Jews, coupled with the animosity surrounding the Samaritan temple, Jesus appears on the scene in Samaritan territory, thus breaking many Jewish cultural taboos. While it may not be completely accurate to classify Samaritans as Gentiles, nevertheless, Jews placed Samaritans within the category.

The New Testament provides at least one reference to a Samaritan as a foreigner (Luke 17:18).[12] Luke records Jesus's astonishment that a foreigner (referring to a Samaritan) was the only cleansed leper who returned to thank him after being healed. Although Jesus portrayed Samaritans favorably, his example seems unsuccessful in changing many of the old prejudices and resentments between the two social groups.
While Jesus had various interactions with Samaritans, two specific stories emphasize the direction the first-century Church had to take in order to spread the gospel throughout the world. One of the stories illustrates Jesus's direct interaction with a Samaritan. In the second illustration, Jesus tells a story, building tension within the parable by inserting a Samaritan as the hero. There is evidence that, at the time, both accounts drew scrutiny from those around Jesus, particularly from the religious elite.

---

[10] Daniel Harrington documents the timeline following the Babylonian conquest and the subsequent period leading up to the Maccabean Revolt. He chronicles the approximate 400-year period from the Jewish exile till the time of the revolt, and the tensions as the result of external rule, which would lead to the revolt. Harrington, *The Maccabean Revolt*, 14-16.

[11] Josephus, *The Works of Josephus*, 352-353.

[12] Nieves and Priest, *This Side of Heaven*, 214.

## The Woman at the Well (John 4:1-45)

John 4 records an interesting event between Jesus and a Samaritan woman, and John's Gospel is the only Gospel to document the event. John introduces the story by using the transitional Greek phrase "ouv," which translates as "therefore, then, or now."[13] John makes this distinction to link the events between chapter 3 and chapter 4. While some scholars may argue that John's transition poses issues regarding chronology, Gerald L. Borchert presents an alternative consideration: "This transition involves matters of substance. Indeed, these verses sounds like an editorial corrective in case anyone might have received the wrong impression that Jesus was merely a baptizing prophet parallel to John the Baptist. The evangelist makes it perfectly clear that such was not the case."[14] John 4:4 presents a peculiar take on the series of events. John states that Jesus "δεῖ"[15] to pass through Samaria. John's emphasis on Jesus's need to travel through Samaria, presents an interesting twist on the movements and thought patterns of Jesus.

First, Jesus initiated the journey because of the Pharisees, the religious elite. John attributes to "the Pharisees," rather than "the Jews," the opposition that indicated the wisdom or necessity of this course.[16] Second, Jews of the day would have avoided traveling through Samaria when traveling from Judea to Galilee by taking the longer route along the river. Unfortunately, the Scriptures do not provide further detail regarding Jesus's necessity.

> Jesus demonstrates that when people set aside
> their cultural differences and engage each other
> in spiritual matters,
> something amazing can occur.

Regardless of Jesus's intent to travel through Samaria, his interaction with the Samaritan woman at the well demonstrates a high level of cultural competency. When he interacts with her, she appears to scoff at

---

13 Thomas, *New American Standard Dictionaries*, Logos.

14 Borchert, *John 1-11*, 198-199.

15 Translated as "had" or "necessary to." Thomas, *New American Standard Dictionaries*, Logos.

16 Spence-Jones, *St. John*, 161.

him for asking her for a drink. Not only was Jesus breaching a cultural barrier by talking with a Samaritan, but he was also conversing with a woman. According to rabbinic teaching, if a woman spoke with a man in public, she could be divorced without having her dowry repaid (Mishnah *Ketubot* 1:8; 7:6). Upon their return from the town, the disciples express surprise and consternation (John 4:27) by the fact that Jesus spoke with a woman, which reinforces the cultural stigma surrounding the interaction. By choosing to engage the Samaritan, Jesus "indicates his esteem for women."[17] However, Jesus goes deeper in his interaction. Not only does he break the cultural barrier by talking to her, but he also engages her in a theological discussion. Aida Besancon Spencer notes, "She is the first person to whom Jesus discloses that he is the Messiah,"[18] and as a result of the interaction, the Samaritan woman "becomes an evangelist to her people."[19]

Jesus's level of cultural competency was not limited to physical understanding. He recognized the deeper spiritual connection between a person's place in this world and his or her standing in eternity. As a result of Jesus's interaction with this tabooed people group, in general, and this stigmatized woman, in particular, God revealed himself to the Samaritans, through his Son, and revival occurred. Jesus demonstrates that when people set aside their cultural differences and engage each other in spiritual matters, something amazing can occur.

## The Good Samaritan (Matt 22:35-40; Mark 12:28-34; Luke 10:25-37)

The story of the Good Samaritan presents another layer in understanding the tension between Jews and Samaritans. It challenges the view that one can divide people into categories of those who are inside the neighborhood of concern and those who are outside.[20] Jesus presents the story in such a manner that the implications reach beyond the traditional Jew/Samaritan feud.

While only the Gospel of John records the interaction between Jesus and the Samaritan woman, variations of the interaction leading up to the story of the Good Samaritan occur in all the Synoptic Gospels. Interestingly, only Luke mentions the actual parable itself. The three

---

17 Spencer, "Jesus' Treatment of Women in the Gospels," 128.
18 Spencer, "Jesus' Treatment of Women in the Gospels," 128.
19 Spencer, "Jesus' Treatment of Women in the Gospels," 128.
20 Hultgren, "Enlarging the Neighborhood," 71-78.

biblical references parallel specifically the exchange between the religious person, identified as an expert in the law, and Jesus. The parable of the Good Samaritan is in what Rudolph Bultmann terms "The Travel Narrative of Luke's Gospel"[21] (between Luke 9:51 and 19:27). Jesus is traveling with his disciples from Galilee to Jerusalem, during which time he instructs his disciples regarding his future departure and engages various individuals and groups along the way. One such encounter seems to appear out of nowhere, "since no location is mentioned."[22]

---

> The story of the Good Samaritan challenges the view that one can divide people into categories—those inside the neighborhood of concern and those outside.

---

Luke 10:25 states: "A lawyer stood up and put him to the test." By introducing this character, Luke signals the reader to expect conflict. The term *lawyer* (νομικός) would not be identical to the modern sense of the word, but rather, an "expert in the Mosaic law."[23] Although the lawyer asks Jesus what appears to be a valid question, the query carried an ulterior motive, which Jesus readily ascertained. Recognizing the man's malign intent, Jesus responds to the lawyer's question with a question; however, in the process, Jesus qualifies his interrogation by asking the lawyer for his own interpretation of the Mosaic Law. The lawyer gives an appropriate Torah response, to which Jesus responds in a seemingly dismissive manner.[24] The lawyer did not want to be dismissed because verse 29 states, "But wishing to justify himself, he said to Jesus, 'And who is my neighbor?'"

With the lawyer's second round of questioning, he reveals his real motive. He was not concerned with the commandment as much as he was with defining the identity of his neighbor. Arland Hultgren dissects the motive of the lawyer: "Who is in, who is out, of the circle of neighbors?

---

21 Bultmann, *History of the Synoptic Tradition*, 177.

22 Hultgren, "Enlarging the Neighborhood," 72.

23 Strahan, "Jesus Teaches Theological Interpretation of the Law," 72.

24 Philip E. Esler, who reads this whole interchange between Jesus and the lawyer as antagonistic, regards Jesus's responses ["What is in the Law? How do you read it?"] not as an actual answer to the lawyer's question about eternal life but as a "sharp and dismissive" challenge, which might be rephrased as "You're a lawyer, what do you think?"; Esler, "Jesus and the Reduction of Intergroup Conflict," 333.

How large is the circle? If it is clear who the neighbor is, it is also clear who is not."[25] In his attempt at self-justification, the lawyer also attempted to differentiate the Jews from Gentiles. His response to Jesus was based on Leviticus 19:18, yet he only quoted the latter half of the verse. The first half of the verse provides clarity regarding the lawyer's motive.[26] In short, a neighbor is a person who belongs to "your people," which in its ancient setting would be a fellow Israelite.[27] By understanding the full content of the verse, the lawyer's motive becomes clear. He wants Jesus to recite the verse from Leviticus, which would mean agreement that one's neighbor was only a fellow Israelite. Discerning the lawyer's motive, Jesus answers his second question with a story. While the characters within the story are unique, the crux of the story lies within the epiphany of the plot twist. Jesus unveils a bombshell when he inserts a Samaritan as "the hero in the story."[28] One can almost hear the gasps from the audience as Jesus speaks the name of the heretics.

Before dissecting the ending of the parable, a literary nuance is worth mentioning. Jesus displays his theology in this parable. An expert in the Mosaic Law has challenged Jesus regarding his interpretation of the Law. One would assume that a crowd was following Jesus, and all ears were turned to what Jesus was going to say. Like the lawyer, the crowd was curious as to who was their neighbor.

---

## The Samaritan's expression of compassion and mercy demonstrates a key focal point in developing cultural competency.

---

In the parable, Jesus disrupts the literary pattern of the text and places the Samaritan's compassion and mercy center stage, as evident from both the structure of the parable as well as from the lawyer's own assessment.[29] The Samaritan's expression of compassion and mercy demonstrates a key focal point in developing cultural competency. The priest and Levite both came, saw, and then passed by on the other side.

---

[25] Hultgren, "Enlarging the Neighborhood," 73.

[26] The complete verse states, "You shall not take vengeance, nor bear any grudge against the sons of your people, but you shall love your neighbor as yourself; I am the Lord."

[27] Hultgren, "Enlarging the Neighborhood," 73.

[28] Strahan, "Jesus Teaches Theological Interpretation of the Law," 80.

[29] Strahan, "Jesus Teaches Theological Interpretation of the Law," 81.

Likewise, the Samaritan came and saw, but then moves toward the victim. Instead of passing by on the other side, the story states that he "had compassion" (Luke 10:33). According to Strahan, this term compassion (σπλαγχνίζομαι) is also used to describe the reaction of the prodigal's father when he sees his son coming from afar, then runs to greet him, kisses him, and restores him to the family.[30] Strahan notes the importance of mercy:

> Even the lawyer picks up on the Samaritan's compassion, for when Jesus asks him, "Who was a neighbor?" the lawyer responds, "The one who demonstrated mercy." Mercy (ελεος), which shares a semantic domain with "compassion," is characteristic of God in Luke. Luke opens his story with two songs that praise God's mercy, the first from Mary who proclaims that God "shows mercy to everyone, from one generation to the next," and the second from Zechariah, who prophesies that God "has shown the mercy promised to our ancestors." Once again, proper interpretation of the Law flows from proper theology.[31]

By inserting the theme of compassion and mercy, Jesus is not simply discussing how one person treats another, but rather communicating a message that connects the audience with a characteristic of God. The connection Jesus is making becomes important when understanding the two greatest commandments, as stated by the lawyer (Luke 10:27).

---

Compassion should lead to action. Culturally competent individuals realize that mere expressions of compassion for people of a different culture are not enough; compassion must propel a person into action.

---

Furthermore, one must examine the disruption in the flow of the story line. The priest and Levite came, saw, and passed by, while the Samaritan came, saw, and had compassion and was moved to action. Compassion should lead to action. Culturally competent individuals realize

---

30 Strahan, "Jesus Teaches Theological Interpretation of the Law," 81.
31 Strahan, "Jesus Teaches Theological Interpretation of the Law," 81-82.

that mere expressions of compassion for people of a different culture are not enough; compassion must propel a person into action.

The details of the Samaritan's actions toward the injured man demonstrate the extensive involvement required when dealing with one's neighbor. Not only did the Samaritan extend compassion, which propelled him to action, but he also exceeded expectations and expressed abundant mercy—all of which provide beautiful reflections of God's own mercy.[32] By touching the injured man, tending his wounds, putting him on his own donkey, and giving generously without expecting repayment, the Samaritan signifies that this man is his neighbor.[33] Jesus's "parable illustrates that proper interpretation of the Law is characterized by compassion, action, and solidarity with the lowly."[34] How ironic that a Samaritan, whose Torah differs from that of his Jewish contemporaries, is nevertheless the model reader of Torah.[35]

While one might assume that the insertion of the Samaritan as the heroic protagonist serves as the twist in the story, perhaps Jesus sought to make another subtle point. The final twist in the plot comes when the hearers insert themselves in the story by asking themselves a question: "Who am I? Am I the priest? Perhaps, am I the Levite? Better yet, maybe I should be the Samaritan? Or, am I the lawyer?" All the stated possibilities are valid for consideration, but they overlook another possible perspective. Mark Allan Powell surmises that the typical American reader will identify himself or herself with either the priest, Levite, or the Samaritan. In essence their conclusion is: "To whom will I be a neighbor?" But Powell poses a different perspective—a perspective that must be consider-ed:

> In short, Jesus challenges his audience (the lawyer) to identify not with any of the three persons who walked down the road … but with the person in the ditch. … The main point of the story is that religious leaders (and by implication all religious people) need to evaluate their faith and life from the perspective of the most marginalized and vulnerable people of the earth. As Luke relates the story, a man who is some kind of religious scholar asks Jesus a theological question, "Who is my neighbor?" This was the sort of question that first-century religious scholars debated in first-century ivory towers. Who is my neighbor? Only Jews? Only

---

[32] Strahan, "Jesus Teaches Theological Interpretation of the Law," 82.

[33] Green, *The Gospel of Luke*, 202-203.

[34] Strahan, "Jesus Teaches Theological Interpretation of the Law," 83-84.

[35] McDonald, "The View from the Ditch," 30.

Torah-observant Jews? … The main point of this parable is not to provide an orthodox answer to one particular question, but to propose an orientation for the consideration of all questions. Jesus suggests that we view the suffering people of the earth not just as "less fortunate" in need of our help, but as teachers whose perspectives and experiences reveal truth that power and privilege obscure.[36]

Powell rightfully provides the vantage point that requires one to deal with the Leviticus 19 passage completely: to love your neighbor *as yourself.* Therefore, "It makes sense that empathy would be dealt with in this parable."[37] Robert Funk comes to the same conclusion, "The narrative picture forces the hearer to take up the position of the one in need of compassion. In so doing he learns what 'as thyself' means."[38] A lack of empathy can be central to the lawyer's interpretive deficiency.[39] Until the hearers take on the vantage point of the person in the ditch, they cannot be empathetic. Consequently, "It is not difficult to hear that behind the lawyer's 'Who is my neighbor?' lurks his real question—'Who is not my neighbor?'—or, more accurately, 'Whom do I not have to love as myself?'"[40]

---

> Until the hearers take on the vantage point of
> the person in the ditch, they
> cannot be empathetic.

---

To successfully develop cultural competency, one must discern the motive behind the questions, and one must understand this: "True empathy leads to compassion, which leads to action."[41] Therefore, compassion without empathy is implied in the lawyer's question, "Whom do I not have to love as myself?" Compassion, empathy, and action cannot be disconnected, because "empathy, compassion, and action are intertwined."[42] Ultimately, cultural competency is demonstrated when we

---

36 Powell. *What Do They Hear?*, 37.
37 Strahan, "Jesus Teaches Theological Interpretation of the Law," 85.
38 Funk, *Language, Hermeneutic, and Word of God*, 219.
39 Strahan, "Jesus Teaches Theological Interpretation of the Law," 85.
40 Green, *Luke*, 314.
41 Funk, *Language, Hermeneutic, and Word of God*, 216.
42 Strahan, "Jesus Teaches Theological Interpretation of the Law," 86.

show empathy and compassion, not just to those who are like us, but empathy and compassion that moves us to action.

# 5

# The Apostolic Tension

While Jesus provides an excellent example of a culturally competent individual, some might argue his divine nature grants an unfair advantage. Therefore, it is imperative to examine other New Testament figures regarding cultural competency. Luke, writer of the Acts of the Apostles, provides interesting insight into the lives of two individuals who may seem similar, but in reality, are not. The Apostle Peter and the Apostle Paul yield an excellent study in contrasting perspectives.

## Peter's Paradigm Shift
## (John 21; Acts 10:1-36)

Acts 10 presents the account of Peter and his interaction with Cornelius, a Roman centurion. If Peter had lived in modern times, people would deem him a racist. A number of biblical references support the claim. While this designation may seem harsh, Peter demonstrates disdain for those of non-Jewish descent. As a result, his influence in the first-century church is affected and could account for his diminished impact in the second half of the book of Acts. This section culminates with the interaction between Peter and Cornelius in Acts 10.

Prior to his ascension, Jesus had an intriguing conversation with Peter (John 21). In the exchange, Jesus asks Peter an interesting question: "Simon son of John, do you love me more than these" (v. 15). Jesus's question to Peter appears to be straightforward. However, Jesus asked Peter the question three times, indicating that either Peter was missing something, or Jesus was emphasizing something important. After each question, Peter responded affirmatively. In the Greek language, there are several words that translate as "love," but in the New Testament two primary words are utilized: *agapé* (ἀγάπη) and *phileó* (φιλέω). The word *agapé* typically refers "to divine love,"[1] whereas Strong defines *phileó* as "intimate friendship."[2] These two words, with distinct definitions, are somewhat similar, yet also different. Both Greek words mentioned are translated into English as "love."

In the dialogue between Jesus and Peter, the word *love* is used six times. Most modern readers interpret each usage of "love" to mean the same thing; however, a review of the Greek text yields a different result: "Jesus uses one word for love in his first two questions *(agape)*, to which Peter responds with a different word *(phileó)*. Jesus's third question and Peter's third answer both use *phileó*."[3] The switch is intriguing, but further inspection reveals that when Jesus asks the question the first time using *agapé*, Peter responds using *phileó* (v. 15). Peter duplicates his response when questioned a second time, which brings the audience to the conundrum in verse 17.

Twice Peter responds to Jesus's *agapé* question with a *phileó* response, so Jesus challenges Peter's *phileó* by questioning him with the response he has been giving. Jesus questions Peter's *phileó* because he knows Peter will have an issue in the very near future. Jesus knows that Peter will struggle when it comes to preaching the gospel to Gentiles. As a result, Jesus challenges Peter: if he at least had a *phileó* level of love for him, he should feed his sheep—all his sheep. Acts 10 reveals Peter's struggle with presenting the gospel to the Gentiles.

## The House of Cornelius

Acts 10 opens with Luke introducing Cornelius, a Roman Centurion, who lives in Caesarea.[4] Luke describes Cornelius as being "a devout man and one who feared God with all his household" (Acts 10:2). By Luke describing Cornelius as devout and one who feared God, or a godfearer, he was demonstrating that "Cornelius already had some preparation for the gospel he was soon to hear."[5] Luke's distinction is important because it lets the audience know that "this centurion was no ordinary Roman soldier. He was deeply religious and actually performed two out of three Jewish acts of piety—prayer and giving of alms."[6]

---

[1] Strong, "*agapé* (ἀγάπη)."

[2] Strong, "*phileó* (φιλέω)."

[3] Strauss, *Four Portraits, One Jesus*, 327.

[4] Unlike Lydda and Joppa, which were mainly inhabited by Jews, Caesarea was a Hellenistic-style city with a dominant population of Gentiles. Polhill, *Acts*, 252.

[5] Polhill, *Acts*, 252.

[6] Gangel, *Acts*, 158.

Unfortunately, there seems to be no indication as to how Cornelius came to faith. Regardless, Luke's story demonstrates the spread of the gospel and its subsequent impact, not only on the Jews but now on the Gentiles.

After Luke's introduction of Cornelius, he documents two separate divine encounters. The first encounter occurred when an angel of the Lord appeared to Cornelius (Acts 10:3). In the second encounter, Peter falls into a trance, and God speaks to him through a vision (vv. 10-16). By placing both divine encounters back-to-back, Luke is communicating that "God interrupts their lives as we have already seen with Ananias and Saul, a sovereign plan to bring them together."[7] Just as God spoke to Peter in John 21, concerning the importance of feeding his sheep, he is now giving Peter the opportunity to live out the charge.

In Peter's vision, God uses the metaphor of Jewish food laws to illustrate how Peter was to interact with the Gentiles.

> Some scholars feel that Peter's vision dealt more with food laws than with interaction with Gentiles. This is to overlook the fact that the two are inextricably related. In Lev 20:24b–26 the laws of clean and unclean are linked precisely to Israel's separation from the rest of the nations. The Jewish food laws presented a real problem for Jewish Christians in the outreach to the Gentiles. One simply could not dine in a Gentile's home without inevitably transgressing those laws either by the consumption of unclean flesh or of flesh that had not been prepared in a kosher, i.e., ritually proper, fashion.[8]

By Luke demonstrating the connection between food laws and Gentiles, he is building upon the words of Jesus when he argued that it was not food that defiled a person, but it was the unclean things in a person's heart (Mark 7:14-23). This was precisely the point of Peter's vision: God declared the unclean to be clean.[9] Just as Jesus was trying to communicate a specific message to Peter in John 21, God still desired for Peter to have a shift in the way he viewed Gentiles. Peter was eventually persuaded to visit Cornelius's house where he has the revelation that "God does not show favoritism but accepts from every nation the one who fears him and does what is right" (Acts 10:34-35).

---

[7] Gangel, *Acts*, 158.
[8] Polhill, *Acts*, 255.
[9] Polhill, *Acts*, 255.

Despite Peter's encounter with Cornelius, it seems that his new revelation was only temporary. The timeframe is unclear, but it appears that the Apostle Paul became aware of Peter's struggle, possibly through another interaction with Christian Gentiles in Galatia. Galatians 2:13 records an exchange in which Paul confronts Peter in Antioch regarding his "hypocrisy"[10] in dealings with the Gentiles. The exchange between Paul and Peter occurred after the events of Acts 10,[11] which indicates that Peter still struggled with cross-cultural ministry despite the revelation that occurred at Cornelius's house. Peter's inability to experience a paradigm shift in his thinking serves as a lesson, one in which we do not emulate the example, but instead we should choose a different path.

---

[10] Wright, *Paul for Everyone*, 21.

[11] There are three primary arguments regarding the date of when Paul wrote Galatians. Regardless of the scenario, all place the writing of Galatians after the exchange in Acts 10. Therefore, there is no dispute regarding the chronology of events. Schreiner, *Galatians Exegetical Commentary on the New Testament*, 138-144; Schnabel, *Acts Exegetical Commentary on the New Testament*, 473-483; Wright, *Paul for Everyone*, 20-23; Bruce, *The Book of Acts*, 201-218.

# Conclusion to Part One

Although the theological foundation of cultural competency may not present itself overtly throughout the Bible, a closer examination of various texts reveals a consistent theme regarding God's view of humankind. In the Old Testament, God created humans as male and female, but did so by creating them in his image. As a result, the *imago Dei* demonstrates that God's creation reflects him, even though he made people different as demonstrated through the gender differentiation in the Genesis 2 creation account.

As the world progresses beyond the creation story, sin is introduced, and it creates a bifurcation between God and his creation. Additionally, as seen in the story of the Tower of Babel, sin even creates a separation between the people in the form of diverse languages. Despite the division, God intervenes and utilizes various individuals to demonstrate cultural competency.

For many centuries, humanity attempted to navigate life but continuously struggled to reconnect with God. Therefore, God demonstrated his love for his people, by sending his son Jesus to come and live amongst humankind. During his life, Jesus exhibits love for people—all people, Jews and Gentiles. How Jesus approached people, regardless of their ethnic background, serves as a model of cultural competency for modern day believers. To truly be followers of Christ, one must embrace the two greatest commandments: To love the Lord our God, with our heart, mind, and soul, and to love our neighbor as ourselves.

# PART TWO

During one's lifespan, a human being faces many complexities. Most people can attest to the complications and challenges of navigating the various stages of life. Personal difficulties present unique challenges, but mix in the social and cultural challenges, and the pressures can be overwhelming. As a result, the role of the pastor takes on a strategic character as he or she assists communities navigating various cultural challenges and nuances.

As American culture continues to morph, pastors face different complications. Ministers not only prepare timely messages and facilitate weekly programming for parishioners, but they must also provide direction and insight for communities dealing with divisive outcomes. The cultural climate in America today presents polarizing issues that divide communities and impact families and churches. The advent of the "BlackLivesMatter" movement has created a stir among the dominant culture in America—White America. The stir has elicited a variety of responses and conclusions, which, again, result in division between friends and family.

As a result of these cultural and social pressures, pastors in the twenty-first century need to develop cultural competency toward various minority groups within their communities. An informal poll of pastors revealed a desire for greater cultural competency but also indicated that pastors admit that they are neither culturally competent nor actively taking steps to develop this necessary competency. This presents a problem.

The following information reflects the results from an informal survey I conducted verbally with a group of pastors in 2016. I surveyed 54 pastors, with 46 responding.

| Question | Yes | No | Not Sure |
|---|---|---|---|
| In your opinion, would you say you are culturally competent? | 13 | 31 | 2 |
| If not, do you know the steps necessary to become culturally competent? | 0 | 35 | 11 |

| If you answered yes to the previous question, are you currently taking steps to increase your cultural competency? | 0 | 0 | 0 |
| --- | --- | --- | --- |

The questions revealed that Pastors desire to understand and minister to the diverse people groups within their communities, but they often simply do not know how to cross the racial divide. As a result of the unanimous response to question 2, the third question wasn't even asked.

This part of the book examines two different (but related) arenas. Chapter 6 first seeks to address why cultural competency matters within the local church. Chapter 7 addresses the impact of increased cultural competency for individuals in the church.

# 6

# Why Cultural Competency Matters

The racial divide is not something new to the American people. The United States of America was established as a result of atrocities to various non-Caucasian people groups, known as minorities. It is important to note that racial inequity does not reside in ancient history. Within the last century, racial and social unrest has continued to manifest at various stages, impacting all facets of American society. The 1990s produced a radical change in terms of the exposure of racial and social injustices in the United States. The advent of the Internet allowed an increased ability for people to access information. Additionally, the upsurgence of the rap music genre exposed the American public to the realities faced by minorities in America, particularly African Americans.

September 11, 2001, seemed to provide some measure of solace, as the country banded together after the attack on the World Trade Center. Americans united as they adjusted to a new reality in the country, the Post 9/11 reality. Following the 9/11 tragedy, American culture seemed to "settle in" to a new normal, as people adjusted to the new security measures present at various public venues through-out the country.

On February 26, 2012, just over a decade after adapting to the "new normal" in America, George Zimmerman shot and killed a Black man by the name of Trayvon Martin.[1] Although countless people have been shot and killed in American history, this particular murder sparked a series of events that led to the introduction of a new movement in American culture now known as "#BlackLivesMatter."[2]

Almost two and a half years later, a police officer in Minneapolis, Minnesota, shot and killed another Black man, Jamar Clark. The outrage

---

[1] CNN Library, "Trayvon Martin Shooting Fast Facts."
[2] Following the acquittal of George Zimmerman, in 2013, for the shooting death of Trayvon Martin, the hashtag "Blacklivesmatter" began trending on social media and led to the Black Lives Matter movement.

from this event caused a flurry of activity to boil over into the community. The Black Lives Matter movement engaged communities in the Twin Cities and sparked people to action. During the Spring of 2016, the Black Lives Matter group organized and held a rally in Elliot Park—one of the communities located on the southeastern edge of downtown Minneapolis. Coincidentally, the Elliot Park neighborhood is home to North Central University (NCU) where I teach, and the park itself is adjacent to the college.

The event in Elliot Park drew massive crowds and engaged people from all over the Twin Cities. Additionally, the protest presented itself, front and center, to the students of NCU, which, in turn, sparked a number of conversations. The subsequent conversations provided the initial impetus for my doctoral work, which then resulted in this book. The reality that many NCU students were uneducated regarding racial and social differences was sobering. Many students even expressed ignorance regarding the subject. While students at NCU receive an amazing education, they appeared to be lacking in cultural competency. Consequently, the task was initiated to create a tool people could use to increase their cultural competency.

Although the quest toward cultural competency may seem noble, a few elements must be understood. These various elements not only provide necessary understanding to move an individual toward becoming more culturally competent, but they also provide context regarding many of the challenges various groups face in America.

## Equality vs Equity

Robert Putnam masterfully purports that the inequality facing young people in America is the result of a socioeconomic gap. Putnam dissects what he calls "Equality of Income and Wealth" and "Equality of Opportunity and Social Mobility."[3] The premise of the issue, as noted by Putnam, stems from the "all men are created equal"[4] statement. However, most Americans are aware that not all people are equal, and they recognize that the disparity between races—and often between men and women— is glaringly obvious. While Putnam's two types of equality are obviously related, because the distribution of income in one generation may affect

---

[3] Putnam, *Our Kids*, 31.
[4] Jefferson, "The Declaration of Independence."

the distribution of opportunity in the next generation, they are not the same thing.[5]

The problem with inequity stems from a misunderstanding of equality versus equity. While 95 percent of Americans agree that "everyone in America should have equal opportunity to get ahead,"[6] Fifty-three percent feel "satisfied with the opportunity for a person in this nation to get ahead by working hard,"[7] which is down from 76 percent in 2001. Americans want everyone to have equality, but they recognize that not everyone can get ahead by simply working hard.

Elizabeth Denevi addresses the tension between equality and equity: "Equality means giving all … the same thing."[8] Denevi then proceeds to contrast equality with equity in terms of education. She poses the idea that, in education, the playing field is not equal: "Equity mandates that we give each student what he or she needs to be successful at school."[9] While Denevi argues her point in relation to secondary and elementary educational systems, the principles behind equality and equity also apply to higher education. The reality exists that while higher education is available to everyone, it may not necessarily be plausible, especially given the various hurdles faced by underprivileged and economically disadvantaged young people, which in turns creates an educational dilemma.

Addressing the educational dilemma by attempting to educate an individual, particularly when it relates to cultural competency, can present many complexities. Julie Landsman, while dealing with the tension of preparing future schoolteachers, addresses the inequity present in higher education:

> U.S. colleges and universities are all over the map in how they prepare young adults to teach in both public and private schools. Some require one week in one semester devoted to identity development, antiracism, and cultural competence. Some barely mention it at all. Without in-depth self-reflection and dialogue around race, Whiteness, cultural competence, White supremacy, and Black history … teachers find themselves lost in classrooms with many students who do not look like them. They come without the knowledge and understanding they so desperately

---

5 Putnam, *Our Kids*, 31.

6 Page and Jacobs, *Class War?*, 57.

7 McCall, *The Undeserving Rich*, 182.

8 Denevi, "What if Being Called Racist," 77.

9 Denevi, "What if Being Called Racist," 77.

need. They do not recognize their lens, the lens they were raised to use to see the world.[10]

Because students lack the knowledge and understanding necessary for cultural competency, the academic world has an opportunity to educate the next generation of leaders. Through the proper dissemination of cultural education, young adults can become self-aware and increase their level of cultural competency. To achieve an increase in cultural competency, individuals must increase their knowledge regarding the formation of culture and the formation of race within the American society. This also requires recognition of one's own cultural misconceptions, which have been impacted by cultural bias. Furthermore, one must also embrace the idea that "being called racist is not the end of the conversation, rather the beginning."[11] While being called racist can be unsettling, it also provides a framework of context necessary for understanding the educational dilemma, in addition to other disparities between racial and ethnic groups.[12]

## Intercultural: The Intersection of Lives

One of the problems when talking about culture is that people use the word in different ways.[13] Culture, as noted by David I. Smith and Pennylyn Dykstra-Prium, is used to describe people groups, geographic locations, forms of artistic expression, and even food:

> It may surprise us to find that the word culture originally meant tilling the land. It is related to the word agriculture. Culture refers to the human activity of transforming our surroundings and making patterns, products, and ways of seeing that in turn shape our sense of self. Culture, in this sense, is not the possession of the few; everyone participates just by being human.[14]

To understand the idea that everyone participates in culture initiates a bifurcation. David Smith discusses the various differences of understanding culture and the issue of cultural misconceptions. When the focus of cultural differences is on "how different cultural groups can live

---

10 Landsman, "The State of the White Woman Teach," 34-35.

11 Denevi, "What if Being Called Racist," 74.

12 The notion of being called racist will be discussed further in the chapter.

13 Smith and Dykstra-Prium, *Christians and Cultural Difference*, 14.

14 Smith and Dykstra-Prium, *Christians and Cultural Difference*, 14-15.

together in the same social or political space, we talk of 'multicultural' matters. When people travel to foreign places and learn to get around, we tend to speak of 'cross-cultural' journeys."[15] While the aforementioned cultural differences are important to understanding culture, Smith proposes a third focus of cultural difference that is paramount to the successful development of cultural competency:

> When we begin to interact with someone whose cultural formation is different from ours, whether at the ends of the earth, in the next valley, or on our own street, and when we attempt to understand one another well, we are involved in "intercultural" interaction. Intercultural describes what happens between cultures. Intercultural learning happens when we learn from one another as our lives intersect.[16]

The intersection of lives is why cultural competency is important. People have a propensity to assimilate with those like their own culture. Smith proposes that through intentional actions, an educational experience occurs, which is paramount to successfully increase one's cultural competence.

## The Invention of Race

Within America, most racial groups fall into one of five categories: White, Black, Hispanic, Asian, or Other. These different racial categories constantly intersect. The interaction is not relegated to the urban centers; rather, multi-racial communities can be found in virtually every city in America. Because cities are no longer homogeneous, America has become what Michael O. Emerson and Christian Smith call a "racialized society."[17] A racialized society, according to Emerson and Smith, is "one in which intermarriage rates are low, residential separation and socioeconomic inequality are the norm, our definitions of personal identity and our choices of intimate associations reveal racial distinctiveness."[18] Sadly, within the racialized society, Glenn Loury points out that "we are never unaware of the race of a person with whom we interact."[19] In a racialized society, race matters for reasons other than merely deciphering someone's

---

[15] Smith and Dykstra-Prium, *Christians and Cultural Difference*, 15.

[16] Smith and Dykstra-Prium, *Christians and Cultural Difference*, 15-16.

[17] Michael Emerson introduces this term. Emerson and Smith, *Divided by Faith*, 7.

[18] Emerson and Smith, *Divided by Faith*, 7.

[19] Loury, *One by One from the Inside Out*, 127.

ethnicity. Emerson and Smith call it "a society wherein race matters profoundly for differences in life experiences, life opportunities, and social relationships."[20]

Emerson and Smith open the door to understanding that people socially construct racial categories. Theodore Allen reinforces Emer-son's assertion by contending that America is "a society that allocates differential economic, political, social, and even psychological rewards to groups along racial lines; lines that are socially constructed."[21] The social construct is not a modern invention; rather it "arose in the sixteenth and seventeenth centuries to justify the overtaking and enslaving of whole people groups."[22] Granted, slavery has since been abolished, but the differentiation of race in America has become an ingrained fabric of the society, thus creating a racially divided culture. Individuals who have darker skin tones have historically been viewed as inferior, thereby creating a caste system in America.

---

To engage in a serious discussion regarding race
in America, one must begin with the flaws of
American society—rooted in historic inequalities
and longstanding cultural stereotypes.

---

As a result, the classification of race within a society means that a natural placement, in terms of a hierarchy, occurred and "is reproduced in everyday actions and decisions."[23] This is why we may define a racialized society, in part, as one that allocates differential rewards by race.[24] Along with rewards, a racialized society will also assign negative monikers meant to stifle and oppress. The common denominator of these views of race is that each still sees Black people as a "problem people," rather than as fellow American citizens with problems.[25]

To engage in a serious discussion regarding race in America, one must begin with the flaws of American society, not with the problems of Black people—flaws rooted in historic inequalities and longstanding

---

20 Emerson, and Smith, *Divided by Faith*, 7.
21 Allen, *The Invention of the White Race*, 79.
22 Allen, *The Invention of the White Race*, 56.
23 Emerson and Smith, *Divided by Faith*, 11.
24 Emerson and Smith, *Divided by Faith*, 8.
25 West, *Race Matters*, 5.

cultural stereotypes.[26] Candid conversation must occur, specifically regarding race, if there is any hope of bridging the racial divide. For individuals striving to increase their cultural competency, the necessity for the conversations increases exponentially. However, to engage in race-based conversations requires intentionality, in addition to understanding some terms. The terms could vary, but one reality must be addressed: "As long as black people are viewed as a 'them,' the burden falls on blacks to do all the 'cultural' and 'moral' work necessary for healthy race relations."[27] Consequently, individuals seeking to increase their cultural competency must first address their own cultural biases and how these biases have fueled various cultural misconceptions.

## Cultural Misconceptions versus Cultural Bias

For people to adequately grow in their understanding of other cultures, they must first address the cultural misconceptions developed because of negative stereotypes and come to grips with the cultural biases that exist within American society. To do so, people must come to terms with the reality "that most of our proposed solutions to racial issues do not work."[28] For generations, Americans have attempted to address the racial divide, and it seems as if no traction has been made since the Civil Rights Movement of the 1960s.

One of the biggest cultural misconceptions is what Gary Weaver calls "The Melting Pot Myth."[29] As best as can be determined, the term "Melting Pot" began circulating in the late eighteenth century.[30] However, the widespread use of the metaphor gained popularity in 1908 following the release of the play, "The Melting Pot," written by Israel Zangwill.[31] The idea behind the concept of the Melting Pot was that all people, regardless of race, were to be considered equal. Like a melting pot, where multiple elements blend to form one whole unit, America was supposed to be a place where everyone could come, and a cultural blending would take place. Weaver makes the follow observation: "We would have to search diligently to find evidence of Chinese, Latin, Middle Eastern,

---

[26] West, *Race Matters*, 6.

[27] West, *Race Matters*, 6.

[28] Emerson and Yancey, *Transcending Racial Barriers*, 8.

[29] Weaver, *Culture, Communication, and Conflict*, 60.

[30] McDonald, *American Ethnic History*, 50.

[31] Wattenberg, "The Melting Pot."

Indian-American, African, or of even Eastern or Southern European ethnic patterns of behavior and thought being absorbed into the American culture."[32] Weaver adequately addresses the majority culture misconception that because various ethnic groups are present in America means that the melting pot exists. While it is true that those various ethnicities are present, the key to consider is the fact that those ethnic group's behaviors and patterns have not been absorbed into the broader American culture.

In 1953, Nathan Glazer published an article under the title, "America's Ethnic Pattern: 'Melting Pot' or 'Nation of Nations'?"[33] Glazer acknowledged that various ethnic groups in America had not maintained their country-of-origin culture but chose instead to shed their old cultures to embrace American culture. Ten years after Glazer's inaugural work, Glazer collaborated with Daniel Moynihan and wrote the book, *Beyond the Melting Pot*, which concluded that the "Melting Pot" did not happen: "Each ethnic group has not contributed its own cultural traits equally to the whole."[34] Instead, American culture has been influenced and dominated by the European-American culture.

Cultural pluralism presents another major misconception within American culture. The concept of the melting pot was predicated and buoyed on the concept that because America incorporates multiple races and ethnicities within its borders, it is culturally pluralistic. That assumption, however, could not be farther from reality. Weaver actually goes as far as to suggest that instead of cultural pluralism, America demonstrated "cultural imperialism."[35] While cultural imperialism might be a stretch, "Assimilation Theory"[36] seems more appropriate. Unfortunately, the assimilation theory requires assimilation of all aspects of a culture, including physical characteristics; therein lies the problem. Perhaps during the early twentieth century, America resembled a culturally pluralistic society, but with the progression of time, cultural norms not assimilated into the greater "White Culture"[37] were received with

---

32 Weaver, *Culture, Communication, and Conflict*, 60.

33 Glazer, "America's Ethnic Pattern, 'Melting Pot' or 'Nation of Nations'?," 401-408.

34 Weaver, *Culture, Communication, and Conflict*, 60.

35 Weaver, *Culture, Communication, and Conflict*, 60.

36 Steinberg, "The Long View of the Melting Pot," 791.

37 According to Richard Dyer, "White Culture" is a broad term characterizing the greater American culture fueled by the oppressive manner of race. He argues that classifying non-whites with a color, and no color for whites, makes non-whites less human. Therefore, the term "white" applies to physical, social, and mental cultural traits found in the dominant culture of America; see Dyer. *White: Twentieth Anniversary Edition*, 1-40.

resistance and stifled. Even if a culture successfully assimilated, the chasm associated with melanin still exists, and the bridge needed to span the crevasse has never been built.

---

> Cultural biases neither occur overnight nor develop as the result of a singular event, but rather occur as the result of historical racial injustices fueled by institutions.

---

While cultural misconceptions apply to American society, as a whole, individuals present unique nuances of cultural biases, but these occur as a result of the misconceptions present within the broader society. Cultural biases neither occur overnight nor develop as the result of a singular event, but rather occur as the result of historical racial injustices fueled by institutions. Cultural biases can only be understood by looking to the past because they "cannot be under-stood by looking at our contemporary racial situation."[38] It is not sufficient to merely confront a racial bias; one must get to the root of the issue by understanding the history and background that created the bias.

One can pursue cultural competency by seeking to understand how history has shaped one's present mindset. Furthermore, under-standing cultural backgrounds provides another important framework for the development of cultural competency. Not only should a person understand the history of racism, which shapes one's biases, but also acquire proficiency regarding how cultural backgrounds have shaped the current context of a particular ethnic group.

## Cultural Backgrounds

To fully come to terms with the history of racism, one should not focus *solely* on the atrocities of racism. Simply studying and recounting the various inhuman acts perpetrated on slaves in America would only produce pity, which leads only to regret. In turn, regret elicits deep emotions, which initiates a sense of vulnerability, thereby increasing the potential for irrational and defensive reactions, which in turn creates a sense of being exposed and helpless. This progression explains why White people become so defensive when issues of race are brought up. Beyond

---

[38] Emerson and Yancey, *Transcending Racial Barriers,* 17.

knowing the past, individuals must be educated regarding their own cultural background and the background of the other culture. In so doing, history provides context and should not only elicit pity.

---

One of the key elements in understanding the history of race in America is to understand the philosophy of
White Supremacy.

---

Books dedicated to the history of America are plentiful, yet not every historical document narrates the horrific events perpetrated on enslaved people of African descent. Many history books do not address the reality that race was an American construct, fueled by the transatlantic slave trade. To fully understand the cultural background of Black history in America, one must grasp how history shaped race, which, in turn, shaped culture. A sociological study, performed by Clem Brooks and Jeff Manza, highlights the split caused by race in American culture.[39] Clem Brooks and Jeff Manza examined many categories, including class, sex, religion, and race, and found that "race was the largest social cleavage," and that the "race cleavage" has actually grown in magnitude since 1960.[40]

Since research indicates that race has caused and continues to cause a divide in American society, this led to the logical conclusion that a thorough study of the history of race in America would prove helpful in developing cultural competency.

One of the key elements in understanding the history of race in America is to understand the philosophy of White Supremacy. Michael Emerson provides a concise summary of its roots:

> The early Africans were imported into the New World as indentured servants. In many ways they were not treated very differently from the European indentured servants who also were brought into the English colonies, although they were perceived as being inferior to whites. However, as the Southern economy became more agrarian based, the need grew, at least in the eyes of the landowners, for individuals who would work as indentured servants indefinitely, who would be enslaved for all of their lives,

---

[39] Brooks and Manza, "Social Cleavages and Political Alignments," 937-946.

[40] Brooks and Manza, "Social Cleavages and Political Alignments," 937-946.

53

and whose children would inherit that status. However, the use of Africans as lifelong slaves required philosophical justification. This justification was soon found in a social construction of racial differences wherein blacks were seen as biologically inferior to whites. This conceptualization led to the ideas that blacks naturally belonged in a subservient position to whites. The development of such stereotypes of Africans and African Americans is an important part of the construction of the white supremacy ideology that dominated U.S. culture for many centuries.[41]

Most White Americans today would shun the creed of White supremacy, primarily because they do not engage in the behaviors prevalent during the slavery era. David Wellman makes the following observation: "Racism is often captured best in people's minds by the ideology and actions of the Ku Klux Klan."[42] Although the Ku Klux Klan embodies the historical symbol of racism, modern forms of racism manifest differently. Emerson clarifies that "racism is viewed as an irrational psychological phenomenon that is the product of individuals, and is evidenced in overt, usually hostile behavior."[43] Based on the definitions of Wellman and Emerson, one would conclude that racism is on the decline, perhaps almost extinct. Therefore, Emerson proposes that "we must adapt our understanding and analysis to the new, post-Civil Rights era."[44] It would seem that as a result of the Civil Rights movement, racism was squelched; however, the roots of systemic injustice still remain intact.

---

> It would seem that as a result of the Civil Rights movement, racism was squelched; however, the roots of systemic injustice still remain intact.

---

Wellman formulates that "Racism is a changing ideology with the constant and rational purpose of perpetuating and justifying a social system

[41] Emerson and Yancey, *Transcending Racial Barriers*, 18-19.
[42] Wellman, *Portraits of White Racism*, 34.
[43] Emerson and Smith, *Divided by Faith*, 8.
[44] Emerson and Smith, *Divided by Faith*, 9.

that is racialized."[45] Racism is not mere individual, overt prejudice, or the free-floating irrational driver of race problems, but the collective misuse of power that results in diminished life opportunities for some racial groups.[46] Therefore, it becomes paramount that an individual who desires to increase his or her cultural competency not only study all aspects of American history, but also dissect the roots of racial division present in the various cultural backgrounds, particularly within one's own narrative and the discourse of the other culture.

## Why Being Called Racist
## is the Beginning

In the process of addressing racism, one confronts the realities posed by cultural misconceptions and cultural biases. Additionally, when individuals delve into the side of American history that seems to be absent in many historical books, they come to terms with the fact that race fueled and continues to fuel division in America. The quest for cultural competency brings an individual face-to-face with a glaring reality—perhaps not so glaring to oneself but glaring to minorities. Denevi came face-to-face with this reality and posed an intriguing question: "What if being called racist was the beginning, not the end, of the conversation?"[47]

---

Racism is not mere individual, overt prejudice, or
the free-floating irrational driver of race
problems, but the collective misuse of power
that results in diminished life opportunities for
some racial groups.

---

White Americans must come to terms with the notion that they are racist. Granted, they may not be the "white hood wearing, cross burning" racists, but rather the racists who benefit from a system meant to elevate Whites and suppress minorities. White Americans must come to understand that they benefit, not because of some overt action on their part, but as the result of simply being White. However, conversations

---

45 Wellman, *Portraits of White Racism*, 41.
46 Emerson and Smith, *Divided by Faith*, 9.
47 Denevi, "What if Being Called Racist," 76.

along the lines of race become uncomfortable for White people. White folks will often say they feel 'unsafe' during conversations regarding race when what they are referring to is a feeling of discomfort.[48] Even when presented with statistics regarding the realities of systemic racism, "whites often either refuse to believe these statistics or, more commonly, find ways to explain them away."[49] It is as if Whites approach the topic of race with an intentional indifference. As a result, White people's voluntary ignorance only widens the racial divide between White culture and Black culture.

---

> White Americans benefit, not because of some overt action on their part, but as the result of simply being White.

---

The reality exists that historically, White Americans have not had to encounter systemic oppression. Therefore, when the dominant culture is presented with a differing perspective, one which emphasizes racist systems that oppress and stifle, the response is one of disbelief. Greg Boyd delineates the rationale behind the skepticism:

> Racist walls pervade the structure of our culture. As a white person, I didn't have to deal with these walls. You see, for all our insistence that America is the land of equal opportunity, there is in fact a stratified 'pecking order' of privilege that is largely structured by one's access to power, social class, ethnicity, and even gender. We think of it as a pyramid of privilege. The higher up the pyramid you are, the fewer walls you have to maneuver around. The lower down the pyramid you are, the more walls you have to maneuver around.[50]

Furthermore, Boyd argues that while many variables can affect where one might land on the pyramid (see below), "all other things being equal, whites (and especially white males) enjoy the privilege of being at the top of the socio-economic pyramid."

---

48 Denevi, "What if Being Called Racist," 77.

49 Boyd, "Racism: Why Whites have Trouble 'Getting It.'"

50 Boyd, "Racism: Why Whites have Trouble 'Getting It.'"

## THE PYRAMID OF PRIVILEGE

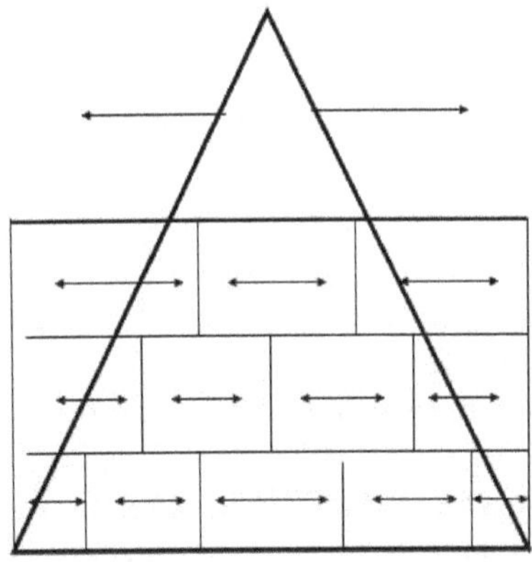

In his article, Greg Boyd illustrates what he terms, "The Pyramid of Privilege."[51] The Pyramid demonstrates what Boyd calls a "pecking order of privilege."[52] This pecking order of privilege is "structured by one's access to power, social class, ethnicity, and even gender."[53] Depending where one might land on the pyramid will dictate the number of walls that the individual will have to navigate, essentially perpetuating a modern day caste system: "The higher up the pyramid you are, the fewer walls you have to maneuver around. The lower down the pyramid you are, the more walls you have to maneuver around."[54] Although many factors can contribute to where one might land on the pyramid, according to Boyd, "whites (and especially white males) enjoy the privilege of being at the top of the socio-economic pyramid."[55] Boyd goes on to explain that White males position at the top of the pyramid exemplifies what has become commonly known as White privilege.

As a result of Boyd's assertion, White Americans must face the foregone conclusion that they are racist. Once they have come to this revelation, they can experience what Brenda Salter McNeil calls a "catalytic event."[56] Catalytic events are not necessarily pleasant experiences, but

---

51 Boyd, "Racism: Why Whites have Trouble 'Getting It.'"
52 Boyd, "Racism: Why Whites have Trouble 'Getting It.'"
53 Boyd, "Racism: Why Whites have Trouble 'Getting It.'"
54 Boyd, "Racism: Why Whites have Trouble 'Getting It.'"
55 Boyd, "Racism: Why Whites have Trouble 'Getting It.'"
56 McNeil, *Roadmap to Reconciliation*, 42.

rather incidents that help "jump-start the reconciliation process."[57] Many White Americans need a jump-start; otherwise, this country will never be able to move forward in terms of racial healing.

---

White Americans must face the foregone
conclusion that they are racist.

---

Therefore, cultural competency education can provide the catalytic event the dominant culture needs. The majority culture needs to understand that as a result of systematic[58] racism, regardless of whether or not they intended to benefit, White Americans have benefitted and continue to benefit. However, while the racist system still exists, it provides an opportunity for the church to become an agent of change—modeling how to increase cultural competency.

---

[57] McNeil, *Roadmap to Reconciliation*, 42.

[58] The word *systematic* was chosen in lieu of *systemic*. Systematic is defined as "having, showing, or involving a system, method, or plan," whereas systemic is defined as "or of relating to a system." Both words speak to the system, but systematic speaks to the planned system. Starting with the transatlantic slave trade, racism has been and is systemic, but it has also been and continues to be systematic. It's not just the systems, but it is the method and plan of those systems that perpetuates racism.

# 7

# Cultural Competency in the Church

"I think it is one of the tragedies of our nation, one of the shameful tragedies, that eleven o'clock on Sunday morning is one of the most segregated hours, if not the most segregated hours, in Christian America."[1] Although Dr. Martin Luther King spoke those words over sixty years ago, they still ring true today. Swedish researcher, Gunnar Myrdal, called this "an American dilemma."[2] The racial divide may never be closed, particularly with White Evangelicals. While White Evangelicals recognize racial issues, they do so with the understanding that prejudices are the problem of individuals as opposed to larger social groups.

The Evangelical Church, particularly the White Evangelical Church, must experience a catalytic event should it ever have hopes of becoming like the church at Antioch, which serves as a biblical example regarding diversity in congregations. In Acts 13:1, Luke not only lists the names of the leaders, but "also provides seemingly random facts. Actually, the specific details about each person listed speak volumes about their ethnicity."[3] Churches will demonstrate cultural competency when the congregants grasp the understanding that they must "empower diverse leaders,"[4] but to do so they must tackle many obstacles, including identifying racism.

## Understanding Racism

The previous chapter addressed the construct of racism and its invention resulting from the transatlantic slave trade. However, defining racism presents many challenges because of how the term has come to be defined. In contemporary society, the term "racism" is interchangeable

---

[1] King, Jr., Interview on "Meet the Press."

[2] Emerson and Smith, *Divided by Faith*, 6.

[3] DeYmaz and Okuwobi, *Multiethnic Conversations*, 169.

[4] DeYmaz and Okuwobi, *Multiethnic Conversations*, 170.

with the word "prejudice." By eroding the definition of racism and allowing the word to encompass prejudice, it presents a false notion regarding what it really means to be racist. Additionally, the now ambiguous nature of racism argues that all "races" can exhibit racism.

---

## The lack of empathy creates a social nuance undetectable to the majority group, but glaringly obvious to the minority.

---

David Wellman provides a good definition of racism: "Racism is analyzed as culturally acceptable beliefs that defend social advantages that are based on race."[5] For Christians to understand racism, they must recognize the social advantages that come as a result of race, which is the point that Greg Boyd is trying to make in the cited article in the previous chapter, "Racism: Why Whites Have Trouble 'Getting It.'" The fact that White Americans have not had to encounter the social barriers that hinder minorities handicaps their ability to even empathize with ethnic groups. The lack of empathy creates a social nuance undetectable to the majority group, but glaringly obvious to the minority.

Unfortunately, American culture has blurred the distinction between racism and prejudice, impacting the argument regarding whether a minority can be racist. Wellman, however, argues, "Racism is not simply bigotry or prejudice; and it should not be confused with ethnic hostilities."[6] To limit racism to an argument concerning one racial group's disdain toward another does not take into consideration the historical, economic, or cultural components of racism. While modern sociologists have focused on the historical, economic, and cultural elements of racism, they have moved away from the psychological. Instead of bringing these components under one conceptual roof, the sociology of racism has been divided into two camps, producing a theoretical bifurcation.[7]

Beverly Tatum argues that while not all racial groups can be racist, they can be prejudiced. Tatum defines prejudice as "a preconceived judgment or opinion, usually based on limited information."[8] Tatum and Wellman both accurately assert that all racial groups can exhibit prejudice,

---

5 Wellman, *Portraits of White Racism*, 4.
6 Wellman, *Portraits of White Racism*, 4.
7 Wellman, *Portraits of White Racism*, 5.
8 Tatum, *Why Are All the Black Kids Sitting Together in the Cafeteria?*, 4.

but not all racial groups can be racist. While prejudice is the disease of the masses, racism is the scourge of the privileged.

---

## All racial groups can exhibit prejudice, but not all racial groups can be racist.

---

Tatum contends that racism could also be defined as "prejudice plus power."[9] Defining racism in such a manner does not emphasize the systemic nature of racism. Without a systemic understanding of racism, one cannot understand the power differential present in Tatum's statement. Power could be conceived on an individual basis, yet "the view that prejudiced individuals are the essence of the race problem of course reflects a focus on the individual as opposed to the larger social units."[10] While racist individuals do exist, to categorize racism around the stereotypical "White Supremacist" distracts from the greater weight of institutional racism, creating a circular deception that many White Americans maintain. Tatum articulates the deception:

> Understanding racism as a system of advantage based on race is antithetical to traditional notions of an American meritocracy. For those who have internalized this myth, this definition generates considerable discomfort. It is more comfortable simply to think of racism as a particular form of prejudice. Notions of power or privilege do not have to be addressed when our understanding of racism is constructed in that way.[11]

Unfortunately, whether White Americans want to acknowledge Tatum's racist world or not, "it is important to understand that the system of advantage is perpetuated when we do not acknowledge its existence."[12] Therefore, when White Americans choose to ignore systemic racism, they might do so because to acknowledge the action risks attaching a racist moniker to a person's identity.

---

9 Tatum, *Why Are All the Black Kids Sitting Together in the Cafeteria?*, 7.
10 Emerson and Smith, *Divided by Faith*, 74.
11 Tatum, *Why Are All the Black Kids Sitting Together in the Cafeteria?*, 9.
12 Tatum, *Why Are All the Black Kids Sitting Together in the Cafeteria?*, 9.

---

Not all White people are bad people. However,
all White people, intentionally or unintentionally,
do benefit from racism.

---

A logical question arises as a result of defining and addressing racism: Are all Whites racist? The question presents a couple dynamics with the inquiry. First, there is an underlying query to the main question: Are all White people bad people? The fundamental question reveals a selfish insecurity within Whites. It reveals a motive that is about how one might be perceived as opposed to how others are treated. The question reveals an egocentric perspective. Still, the secondary question needs to be answered, because the answer reveals the second dynamic to the initial question. Not all White people are bad people. However, all White people, intentionally or unintentionally, do benefit from racism.[13] The previous statement invokes the second dynamic to the original question: What are White people as individuals doing to impede racism? Because racism is so ingrained in the fabric of American institutions, it is easily self-perpetuating.[14] All that is required is business as usual.[15]

The church is not exempt from pervasive racism. Dr. King recognized the fingerprint of racism and spoke out against it. Unfortunately, "many Christians remain simply apathetic, ignorant, or refuse to admit any problems exist."[16] The disregard demonstrated by the church is rooted in the ethos of early Pentecostal leaders. Frank Bartleman, an eyewitness and participant of the Azusa Street revival, "constantly appealed to history, concluding that whenever the church became enmeshed in the concerns of the State, the life and message of the church were compromised."[17] Bartleman, and others with a similar motif, influenced the formation of the modern Pentecostal Church by leveraging the message to influence ecclesiology.

Nevertheless, the modern church should not lose heart. Hope has not faded. In fact, Emerson and Smith make an encouraging statement: "Religion has tremendous potential for mitigating racial division and

---

[13] Tatum, *Why Are All the Black Kids Sitting Together in the Cafeteria?*, 11.

[14] Rothenberg, *Race, Class, and Gender in the United States*, 332.

[15] Tatum, *Why Are All the Black Kids Sitting Together in the Cafeteria?*, 11.

[16] Mattson, "Social Justice is a Christian Tradition."

[17] Bartleman, "Last Day Conditions," 4.

inequality."[18] If the modern church can embrace the perspective that Whites benefit from systemic racism, they will experience their own catalytic event as a result of the revelation. The revelation will allow the church to embark upon a journey to overcoming some of the key obstacles for not only becoming more culturally competent, but also overcoming obstacles related to facilitating a multi-cultural church.

## Keys to Overcoming Obstacles

Achieving cultural competency will require time, hard work, and commitment. The task will not be easy, and the path that must be walked will yield many volatile twists and turns. The mission focuses on bridging the dividing walls of hostility that are tearing our world apart.[19] The church needs a plan to address the racial divide present within its four walls because ethnic diversity does not occur organically, but rather requires strategic initiation, planning, and implementation.

Topics related to race are difficult and messy and can create tension and foster feelings of frustration. While one might argue that perhaps race would be easier to address if it were avoided all together, but people know there is something better and that they ought to pursue it.[20] The modern church must embrace and integrate a few key components in their efforts to increase cultural competency and bridge the racial divide. The first key component focuses on entering the quest for understanding differing social environments.

## Understanding Social Environments

Communities still experience a great deal of social segregation.[21] The Sunday morning apartheid manifests because of the lack of under-standing when it comes to differing social environments. If the White Evangelical Church has any hope of bridging the racial divide, they need to understand the social differences and embrace an ethos that highlights all cultural social environments. But to do so, the church must acquire a level of understanding regarding social environments. In essence, the corporate church must increase their cultural competency. For the modern church to become an Antioch Church, they must come to terms with

---

18 Emerson and Smith, *Divided by Faith*, 153.
19 McNeal and Richardson, *The Heart of Racial Justice*, 24.
20 Emerson and Yancey, *Transcending Racial Barriers*, 11.
21 Tatum, *Why Are All the Black Kids Sitting Together in the Cafeteria?*, 4.

racism that exists in the church. An unwillingness to address racism will only continue to benefit White America and will only further segregate the church.

One of the first components necessary to understanding different social environments is to recognize that "your way is just [*a*] way and not the [*the*] way."[22] Ethnocentrism presents itself in the "my way" mentality. In the church, ethnocentrism readily manifests itself with music. One need not perform extensive research to recognize that within the last 100 years, musical styles and preferences vary exponentially between White and Black America. White America usually does not understand that African American music is one of the only, if not the only, cultural aspects they were able to preserve throughout slavery and beyond.

Slaveholders limited or prohibited education of enslaved African Americans because they feared it might empower their chattel and inspire or enable emancipatory ambitions.[23] The educational restriction forced these enslaved people to utilize other methods to preserve their history and culture. As a result, "African oral traditions, nurtured in slavery, encouraged the use of music to pass on history, teach lessons, ease suffering, and relay messages."[24] For African Americans, music is more than entertainment; it encompasses history and embodies their culture. In African American churches, music is not relegated to five songs at the beginning of the service, but is integrated into every aspect of the service, including the preaching. White Evangelicals do not understand the importance of musical elements that are paramount for African Americans in church services. Again, it is not simply about music, it is about culture and history. Therefore, addressing the musical components of a church service should be one of the first, if not the first, items a church addresses as it seeks to bridge the racial divide in modern worship.

Another element with glaring differences between the White and Black church in America is their view and treatment of the pastor. Congregants within the Black church revere, respect, and place their pastor on a pedestal—almost in line with the matriarchal figure within the Black family structure. In contrast, congregants in White churches view their pastors as employees who can be hired and fired at will and who exist to serve their needs. The differing perspective presents a massive disunion in the modern church. A survey of thirty-two African American pastors, and

---

22 DeYmaz and Li, *Leading a Healthy Multi-Ethnic Church*, 126.
23 "Celebrating African American Culture & History."
24 "Celebrating African American Culture & History."

fifty-four Caucasian pastors confirmed the cultural assessment regarding how congregants view Black and White pastors.[25]

HOW CONGREGANTS VIEW THEIR PASTORS

| | Yes | No | Not Sure |
|---|---|---|---|
| 1. Are you a pastor at a church? | 91% | 9% | |
| | **Caucasian** | **African-American** | **Other** |
| 2. What is your ethnic background? | 54% | 32% | 5% |
| | **Primarily White** | **Primarily Black** | **There is no discernible dominant ethnic group** |
| 3. What is the demographic make-up of your church? | | | |
| **Caucasian Respondents** | 74% | 19% | 7% |
| **African-American Respondents** | 16% | 78% | 6% |
| | **More favorably** | **Less favorably** | **I am not sure** |
| 4. In your opinion, are White pastors viewed more/less favorably by White parishioners? | | | |
| **Caucasian Respondents** | 35% | 57% | 7% |
| **African-American Respondents** | 25% | 69% | 6% |
| **Other Respondents** | 80% | 0% | 20% |
| | **More favorably** | **Less favorably** | **I am not sure** |
| 5. In your opinion, are Black pastors viewed more/less favorably by Black parishioners? | | | |
| **Caucasian Respondents** | 70% | 19% | 11% |
| **African-American Respondents** | 88% | 3% | 9% |
| **Other Respondents** | 100% | 0% | 0% |

The survey acknowledged that 87.5 percent of Black respondents, and 70.4 percent of White respondents agreed that Black congregants viewed their pastor more favorably than White congregants. Additionally, 68.75 percent of Black respondents concluded that White congregants view their pastor in a less favorable light, compared with Black congregations, while 57.4 percent of White respondents maintained the same result.

---

[25] Adam Sikorski, "How Congregants View Their Pastors," Survey, October 26, 2018.

> Ultimately, proper education, fueled by cultural
> competency, presents the
> only real solution to the dilemma.

In addition to intentionality regarding cultural diversity within their congregations, pastors also need to address their congregants' perspective regarding their pastor. Neither viewpoint should be viewed as more proper than the other, but rather congregants should pursue a middle ground between the conflicting perspectives. Intentional actions by church leaders can bring about the changes necessary for successful multi-cultural setting. Ultimately, proper education, fueled by cultural competency, presents the only real solution to the dilemma.

## Increasing Cross-Cultural Effectiveness

Social settings present unique challenges due to the variety of cultural norms. When one adds the variable of race and ethnicity, the variants increase exponentially. While a church cannot physically assimilate the many social settings present in a diverse congregation, it can incorporate key components important to the different cultural groups. Churches that intentionally address issues regarding a variety of social settings will increase their cross-cultural effective-ness.

**First, a church must clearly articulate the reason for being intentional regarding cross-cultural effectiveness.** The complexity and variety of the culture of the Christian church allows for a wide variety of expressions of evangelistic ministry.[26] Therefore, congregants need context regarding the strategies integrated into the church. Unfortunately, churches integrate strategies without intentionality regarding cultural pluralism.

Mark DeYmaz addresses the need for cross-cultural intentionality by prescribing three biblical reasons why the church should increase its cross-cultural efforts:

> Jesus envisioned the multiethnic church, for the sake of the gospel, on the night before he died (John 17:2-3, 20-23). Luke

---

[26] Lingenfelter, *Agents of Transformation,* 22.

described the multiethnic church in action, at Antioch, as a model for future congregations to follow (Acts 11:19-26; 13:1-3). Paul prescribed the multiethnic church in order to advance a credible witness of God's love for all people (Eph. 2:11-4:6; 3:2, 6).[27]

DeYmaz's reasons, which align with the New Testament model for the church, need to be understood as the "why." Without a biblical "why," the church will not experience the outcomes exemplified by the first-century church model. The Early Church understood that "it's about reconciling men and women to God through faith in Jesus Christ, and about reconciling a local church to the principles and practices of New Testament congregations of faith."[28] Ultimately, the "why" supersedes selfish motives and focuses on a greater purpose. The church no longer emphasizes the individual, but rather pinpoints the goal of restoring humanity back to a right relationship with God.

**Second, the church must identify the disparate social dynamics present within their ministry.** To do so, one should consider the "five ways of life"[29] articulated by anthropologists Michael Thompson, Richard Ellis, and Aaron Wildavsky in their book, *Cultural Theory*: (1) hierarchy, (2) egalitarianism, (3) fatalism, (4) individualism and (5) autonomy.

Thompson, Ellis, and Wildavsky propose a theory regarding cultural bias and social relations. They define cultural bias as "shared values and beliefs"[30] and define social relations as "patterns of interpersonal relations."[31] Based on these two definitions, they further explain that "When we wish to designate a viable combination of social relations and cultural bias we speak of a way of life."[32] Their assertion is that people group's "way of life" is governed by social relations and cultural bias. The governance of the way of life is presented as the theory of "sociocultural viability."[33] Essentially, sociocultural viability "explains how ways of life maintain (and fail to maintain) themselves."[34] To simplify the above stated

---

27 DeYmaz and Okuwobi, *Multiethnic Conversations,* 13.

28 DeYmaz and Li, *Leading a Healthy Multi-Ethnic Church,* 37.

29 Thompson, Ellis, and Wildavsky, *Cultural Theory,* 1.

30 Thompson, Ellis, and Wildavsky, *Cultural Theory,* 1.

31 Thompson, Ellis, and Wildavsky, *Cultural Theory,* 1.

32 Thompson, Ellis, and Wildavsky, *Cultural Theory,* 1.

33 Thompson, Ellis, and Wildavsky, *Cultural Theory,* 1.

34 Thompson, Ellis, and Wildavsky, *Cultural Theory,* 1.

theory, the anthropologists opted for the simpler phrase, "Cultural Theory"[35] to the explain the concept.

The authors say in *Cultural Theory* that the five ways of life—(1) hierarchy, (2) egalitarianism, (3) fatalism, (4) individualism, and (5) autonomy—are present in every civilization, including America. These ways govern and dictate social life and social change. The problem is addressing a means to change from one way of life to another. Interestingly, the book argues that "Introducing more than two modes of organizing social life make social change both more difficult and more interesting to explain."[36] The book points to why racism, and specifically the racial divide, still exists and has essentially existed for all of human history.

---

> Because systems and institutions continue to benefit from systemic racism, the alternatives will not be pursued. Therefore, system and institutional mindsets must be addressed on a large scale; otherwise, attempts to switch the way of life will be met with futility.

---

Change within a society requires the implementation of particular methods in order to achieve said results. The thought is, "Change occurs when successive events intervene in such a manner as to prevent a way of life from delivering on the expectations it has generated, thereby prompting individuals to seek more promising alternatives."[37] Although it would appear that American society is at the point where they are seeking more promising alternatives, the fallacy is that the established way of life is no longer delivering on its expectations. Thus, the perpetuation of systemic racism occurs. Because systems and institutions continue to benefit from systemic racism, the alternatives will not be pursued. Therefore, system and institutional mindsets must be addressed on a large scale; otherwise, attempts to switch the way of life will be met with futility.

---

[35] Thompson, Ellis, and Wildavsky, *Cultural Theory*, 15.

[36] Thompson, Ellis, and Wildavsky, *Cultural Theory*, 3.

[37] Thompson, Ellis, and Wildavsky, *Cultural Theory*, 3-4.

# The Five Ways of Life

Following is a description of each of the five ways of life, as outlined in *Cultural Theory*. Each way of life hinges on the concept that social control is a form of power. Therefore, whoever controls the social environments is, in essence, in a position of power. The five ways of life illustrate the social dynamics at work within a society—including American society. Any attempted breech or deviation from the existing social dynamics is played out through what the book terms the social game. However, to understand the social game, the five ways of life must be defined.

*Hierarchy*

> When an individual's social environment is characterized by strong group boundaries and binding prescriptions, the resulting social relations are hierarchical. Individuals in this social context are subject to both the control of other members in the group and the demands of socially imposed roles.[38]

The hierarchical approach has governed much of human civilization throughout history. It seems that people have always been subjugated to others in authority, which means the practice has become a social norm, at least, until it is taken too far.[39] Ironically, the reason the hierarchical way of life succeeds is because "the exercise of authority (and inequality more generally) is justified on the grounds that different roles for different people enable people to live together more harmoniously than alternative arrangements."[40] For some unexplained reason, throughout history, people have accepted that differing people should accept differing roles in the society. While on the surface, the notion appears succinct, below the surface, ruling fractions oppose the groups they oversee, thereby creating major problems.

---

38 Thompson, Ellis, and Wildavsky, *Cultural Theory*, 6.

39 To name of few examples in history of when human subjugation was taken too far: (1) the Jews enslaved in Egypt at the beginning of the book of Exodus, (2) the mass genocide of Jews at the hands of Nazi Germany, and (3) the mass enslavement of Africans to fuel the growth and expansion of colonial America.

40 Douglas, "Cultural Bias," 191.

*Egalitarianism*

"Strong group boundaries coupled with minimal prescriptions produce social relations that are egalitarian."[41] Initially, egalitarianism appears to be the preferred social construct. However, within this way of life exists a major flaw. Within the group dynamic, there is no "internal role differentiation,"[42] which means relationships between members are undefined. As a result, authority can only be granted through a form of manipulation—by essentially choosing to "speak in the name of the group." The result is that the self-proclaimed spokesmen can only be dethroned if they are expelled from the group, which sounds a lot like anarchy.

*Individualistic*

"Individuals who are bound by neither group incorporation nor prescribed roles inhabit an individualistic social context. In such an environment all boundaries are provisional and subject to negotiation."[43] This way of life appears to offer a path that is free of control from others. However, "that does not mean the person is not engaged in exerting control over others."[44] Therein lies the problem with this way of life. In fact, "the individualist's success is often measured by the size of the following the person can command."[45] While the notion that a person is not subjugated to the demands of others within the individualistic framework does not warrant that the person, in turn, would become the oppressor by exerting control over others.

*Fatalistic*

"People who find themselves subject to binding prescriptions and are excluded form group membership exemplify the fatalistic way of life. Fatalists are controlled from without."[46] Fatalistic people are similar to those in a hierarchical way of life in that their "individual autonomy is restricted."[47] They are different from those in a hierarchical way of life in

---

41 Thompson, Ellis, and Wildavsky, *Cultural Theory*, 6.

42 Thompson, Ellis, and Wildavsky, *Cultural Theory*, 6.

43 Thompson, Ellis, and Wildavsky, *Cultural Theory*, 7.

44 Thompson, Ellis, and Wildavsky, *Cultural Theory*, 7.

45 Douglas, "Cultural Bias," 206-207.

46 Thompson, Ellis, and Wildavsky, *Cultural Theory*, 7.

47 Thompson, Ellis, and Wildavsky, *Cultural Theory*, 7.

that they are "excluded from membership in the group,"[48] thereby limiting their ability to make decisions geared toward dictating their life.

*Autonomy*

The fifth way of life presents itself in a completely different manner. "The individual withdraws from coercive or manipulative social involvement altogether. This is the way of life of the hermit, who escapes social control by refusing to control others or to be controlled by others."[49] Ironically, in theory, the autonomous way of life is the desired social outcome. The notion being, that people could live in such a way that they are not controlled by others nor do they control others. Unfortunately, the hermit's self-sufficient approach does not lend any contributions to the greater society, thus rendering them into a position of isolation and ineffectiveness.

~

Sherwood Lingenfelter summarizes the anthropologists' characteristics of social and cultural experience by saying, "These five ways of life are generated by a congruence between particular patterns of social and interpersonal relationship and patterns of shared values and beliefs."[50] While patterns exist, cultural groups are not in tandem with each other, which is why cultural bifurcations exist within the church. Therefore, simply identifying the different social dynamics cannot be sufficient for a church; they must seek to rectify the differences between each cultural group.

***

Cultural biases need to be
acknowledged and resolved.

***

To remedy the differences, Thompson, Ellis, and Wildavsky contend that cultural biases need to be acknowledged and resolved: "The cultural bias of each game prototype stems from a distinctive way of looking at the world."[51] Within social games, groups will embrace a particular preference based on the myths of blame, envy, scarcity, risk, and other dimensions of social value. While the anthropologists assign these

---

[48] Thompson, Ellis, and Wildavsky, *Cultural Theory*, 7.
[49] Thompson, Ellis, and Wildavsky, *Cultural Theory*, 7.
[50] Lingenfelter, *Agents of Transformation*, 23.
[51] Thompson, Ellis, and Wildavsky, *Cultural Theory*, 56.

traits to communities, they also provide insight for the church. Lingenfelter expounds on a concept presented by Thompson, Ellis, and Wildavsky: "[In] Small-scale communities, social pressure tends to eliminate competing games. But, as population increases, larger-scale societies allow greater social choice, which results in individual and group variability."[52] Lingenfelter's assessment explains why smaller churches tend to be more unified than their larger counterparts because there is less chance of differing social dynamics. Larger churches, by the sheer size of the congregation, have a propensity for the presence of many more social dynamics. As a result, the complexities related to embraced social preferences render an exponential number of social differences, which in turn generates a greater potential for various ramifications; good or bad.

Lingenfelter's conclusion manifests specifically in church growth. As churches grow, they navigate many complexities as a result of the growth. Add in differing perspectives based on the various "social games," and conflict is generated. However, churches should not fear or avoid dealing with the conflict, but rather create and cultivate outlets of expression and conversation.

---

> Churches should not fear or avoid dealing with conflict, but rather create and cultivate outlets of expression and conversation.

---

Unfortunately, the modern world has embraced the lie that to disagree with someone also means despising them. Differing perspectives provide differing conclusions. It is not the church's job to validate or refute a cultural group's conclusion, but rather to provide social settings for differing groups to interact and disseminate opposing values—to provide a framework for change. Interestingly, Lingenfelter suggests "that society is dynamic, with people creating variants of the game prototypes or even shifting from one social game to another."[53] As a result, one can reasonably conclude that cross-cultural effectiveness will emerge when the redemptive and transformative work of the Holy Spirit is inserted into social dynamics.

The third and final key to cross-cultural effectiveness focuses on relying on the power of the Holy Spirit. The church needs to understand that "racism and ethnic strife are ultimately spiritual problems that demand

---

[52] Lingenfelter, *Agents of Transformation,* 30.
[53] Lingenfelter, *Agents of Transformation,* 31.

spiritual solutions … so that we can minister more effectively to the emerging culture."[54] The church cannot minimize the role of the Holy Spirit, but rather must embrace the biblical message of transformation that comes through the Holy Spirit. Ultimately, this will bring about sociocultural change.

The Holy Spirit played an important role in early Black theology. William Turner points out that while "pneumatology was implicit, but understated,"[55] enslaved people of African descent understood that "calling the name of Jesus amounted to an invocation of the Spirit. The sense was that Jesus is the pneumatic Christ."[56] Because they dreamed about eventual emancipation, they made a connection between the liberation that would come through deliverance and freedom in the Spirit. The prophetic sense was that God was going forth into the world to establish justice and to cause the faithful believer to know the vindication that has been promised.[57] They also resonated with the plight of the Jewish people in the Old Testament, which meant that they, like the Jews, slaves longed for God to deliver them from bondage.

In the Old Testament, sin separated humankind from God. In the New Testament, Jesus's death and subsequent resurrection allowed humanity the opportunity to come back into a personal relationship with God. In addition to the relational restoration experienced as a result of Jesus Christ, in the Book of Acts, the first-century church experienced the Holy Spirit, who continued the restorative work of Christ. Throughout the Book of Acts, the work of the Holy Spirit is seen through the unification of the Body of Christ. Salter-McNeil beautifully states the realization made by the Apostles: "It takes the Holy Spirit to melt down the inner barriers we have erected and to create in us a desire for God and for other people. This is not humanly manufactured. We can't do it by ourselves. It takes a work of God's grace in our lives."[58] Lasting change requires God's grace, manifested through the Holy Spirit, in the lives of believers.

Lingenfelter masterfully illustrates how the biblical message can impact the Church so it can experience effective ministry:

> The message of transformation is neither individualist nor hierarchist, neither authoritarian nor egalitarian. The Great Commandment is to love the Lord our God with all our heart, all

---

54 Salter-McNeil and Richardson, *The Heart of Racial Justice*, 52.

55 Turner Jr., "Pneumatology," 171.

56 Turner Jr., "Pneumatology," 171.

57 Turner Jr., "Pneumatology," 171.

58 Salter-McNeil, *The Heart of Racial Justice*, 61.

our soul, all our mind, all our strength, and to love our neighbors as ourselves. The message of salvation is a message of faith in the person and work of the Lord Jesus Christ. It is not a call to a particular set of social relations or to a particular cultural bias. No cultural bias or set of social relationships is untouched by the unconventional ideas of the gospel.[59]

In fact, the gospel presents a new paradigm, a pattern that does not differentiate based on race or ethnicity, but rather on one's identity in Christ. To fully understand one's identity in Christ, one should understand the theology of *imago Dei*, as outlined earlier in this book. Because humankind is created in God's image (*imago Dei*), Christians need to understand that God's image is not predicated solely on His image in the singular sense, but rather in the triune sense—God the Father, God the Son, and God the Holy Spirit. To fully integrate a holistic view, in conjunction with *imago Dei*, people cannot fully understand "who they are" until they understand that the Holy Spirit plays an important of a role in shaping their identity.

---

### As the Holy Spirit begins to help people understand who they are, cultural competency comes into view.

---

As the Holy Spirit begins to help people understand who they are, cultural competency comes into view. Additionally, "Pentecost is in fact the divine, public act of a free and liberating radical inclusion of differences mediated by the Holy Spirit."[60] As believers come to fully understand their identity as a child of God, they will begin to view other people as children of God regardless of their ethnic background. The transformative work of the Holy Spirit in a believer's heart will also transform his or her perspective of other people. However, the sustainability of cultural competency requires an understanding of cultural humility.

---

[59] Lingenfelter, *Agents of Transformation*, 230.
[60] Medina, *Christianity, Empire and the Spirit*, 353.

# Cultural Humility

Ironically, the very pursuit of cultural competency could also lead to its own demise. The goal of becoming culturally competent should be understood in light of long-term sustainability as opposed to merely arriving at a destination. Recent developments in the field of cultural competency have unearthed a manner in which cultural competency could be sustainable and continue to morph as cultures develop.

Recent research and conclusions have revealed a paradigm shift regarding understanding cultural competency. While cultural competency should be the pursuit, there are limitations to the inquiry. The present shortcoming to cultural competency hinges on the balance between pursuing knowledge to increase a person's cross-cultural effectiveness or succumbing to a cultural hubris mentality, which will only perpetuate and reinforce racism. True cultural competency must also recognize that people and cultures continuously change.

> The goal of becoming culturally competent should be understood in light of long-term sustainability as opposed to merely arriving at a destination.

In an article published by the *Journal of Counseling Psychology*, the contributors offer a new prototype referred to as "cultural humility."[61] The article suggests that cultural humility is the "ability to maintain an interpersonal stance that is other-oriented (or open to the other) in relation to aspects of cultural identity that are most important to the [person]."[62] While cultural humility should incorporate an "other-oriented" approach, a deeper understanding of the terminology needs to be explored.

Cultural humility is better understood, not from the perspective of the other person as explained by the authors of the article in the *Journal of Counseling Psychology* but rather from the person striving for cultural competency. Therefore, a more appropriate explanation of cultural humility emerges. In an article published by the National Mentoring

---

[61] Hook, "Cultural Humility," 354.
[62] Hook, "Cultural Humility," 354.

Partnership about mentoring young men of color, the Partnership effectively extrapolates the context of cultural humility:

> The term "cultural competence" has been used to describe an individual's competency in understanding race and understanding one's own biases. The term "cultural humility" highlights the notion that one is never done when it comes to cultural understanding. One doesn't reach a level of competence and become an expert. Cultural humility supports the notion that we should always be listening, learning, and reflecting.[63]

Therefore, pastors ought to acknowledge the need for continuous education regarding cultural differences rather than thinking they have achieved a certain level of competence regarding a different culture. When it comes to engaging culture and exploring an individual's cultural identity, humility is a great tool and represents a worthwhile place to begin.[64] All pastors should take a position of humility as they minister—whether through messages preached from the pulpit, staff and leadership trainings, or enterprises initiated through engagement in the community.

---

[63] The National Mentoring Partnership and My Brother's Keeper Alliance, "Guide to Mentoring Boys and Young Men of Color," 6.
[64] Hook and Davis, *Cultural Humility*, 2.

# Conclusion to Part Two

The vocational demands of a pastor are complex, varied, and sometimes convoluted, all of which could cause a pastor to refrain from tackling the delicate details necessary to develop cultural competency. Additionally, the pursuit of cultural competency presents multiple navigational challenges. One should not lose heart, despite the political and systemic forces ingrained in American culture that complicate the pursuit of cultural competence.

The time has come for current and future pastors to embrace the call to be more competent regarding other cultures. As Sir Winston Churchill exclaimed,

> There comes a certain moment in everyone's life, a moment for which that person was born. That special opportunity, when he seizes it, will fulfill his mission—a mission for which he is uniquely qualified. In that moment, he finds greatness. It is his finest hour.[1]

It is time for the church to seize upon an opportunity to effect change within American communities; it is time for the church's finest hour.

Just as American society and culture has changed, so has vocational ministry training. While certain methods stand the test of time, the dawning of a new era of ministers has come. Ministers in the Common Era must learn to minister cross-culturally, but to do so they must become more culturally competent. Part three of this book moves toward practical integration by walking through a series of strategic encounters, fueled by a cultural competency assessment, with the goal of increasing one's cultural competency.

---

[1] Churchill, Optimize.me.

# PART THREE

Developing cultural competency presents many complexities. Primarily, people encounter difficulty in knowing how to achieve the objective. Individuals who have expressed a desire to increase their cultural competency also indicate that they do not know what to do to move from point A to point B. To address these issues, I propose practical steps that anyone can take to increase his or her cultural competence.

I have been on my own cultural competency journey since I first stepped foot in the city of Detroit in 1993 for my first ministry assignment. During my time there, I became painfully aware of my own personal biases and was forced to deal with many heart issues related to race. While my time in Detroit did not solve all my cultural competency shortcomings, it did set me on a path toward self-discovery, which is paramount to becoming more culturally competent.

Around 2017 during a period of inquiry on cultural competency, I was introduced to the Intercultural Development Inventory (IDI) assessment, which provides a means of measuring cultural competency. It also provided a roadmap by which to achieve the goals of this project. Since that time, I have become a certified IDI facilitator, further propelling me down the path of my own cultural competency journey.

Utilizing my experiences and research, coupled with the knowledge gleaned from the IDI assessment, the following chapters will provide practical steps for anyone to increase their cultural competency.

# 8

# The Intercultural Development Inventory (IDI)

As a part of the research for this book, I reviewed several different cultural competency assessment tools, but I decided to use the IDI for a few primary reasons. First, I chose the IDI because of its cross-cultural validity, reliability, and generalizability measure of intercultural competence along the validated intercultural development continuum (adapted, based on IDI research, from the DMIS theory developed by Milton Bennett).[1]

The other assessments I reviewed were based on measuring individual Cognitive/Affective/Behavioral (CAB) concepts, by measuring components such as open-mindedness. This is important to growing in cultural competence, but the assessments lacked in the area of goal accomplishments in culturally diverse settings. Essentially, individuals could progress in cultural competency without physically injecting themselves into a cultural setting different than their own.

In contrast, the IDI emphasized learning opportunities geared toward inserting the individual into real scenarios, forcing them to physically engage with different cultural settings.

The second reason why I selected the IDI was because of its breadth in allowing integration with any attempts at cultural competence, regardless of the person's own ethnic heritage and the ethnic milieu of the group to which the person wanted to increase in cultural competency. Regardless of one's definition of racism, cultural competency should be everyone's endeavor no matter their race or ethnic background. Ultimately, I wanted an assessment that could be utilized regardless of a person's ethnicity or level of cultural competency.

---

[1] IDI, "The Roadmap to Intercultural Competency Using the IDI."

Third, the learning opportunities emphasized in the IDI provided a framework to develop a program utilizing the extensive research that fuels the IDI. The IDI also provides a history of success in terms of individuals who have successfully increased their cultural competency. The learning opportunities provide the participant with the occasion to experience their own catalytic moment, which is necessary to embark on the journey.

Fourth, I chose the IDI simply because of the approval that I received from the people with whom I consulted in the process. Those people's validation solidified the decision for me.

## IDI Introduction

The following information provides general information related to the IDI.

The Intercultural Development Inventory® (IDI®) is the premier cross-cultural assessment of intercultural competence that is used by thousands of individuals and organizations to build intercultural competence to achieve international and domestic diversity and inclusion goals and outcomes. IDI research in organizations and educational institutions confirms two central findings when using the IDI:

*Interculturally competent behavior occurs at a level supported by the individual's or group's underlying orientation as assessed by the IDI.*

*Training and leadership development efforts at building intercultural competence are more successful when they are based on the individual's or group's underlying developmental orientation as assessed by the IDI.*

In contrast to many "personal characteristic" instruments, the IDI is a cross-culturally valid, reliable, and generalizable measure of intercultural competence along the validated intercultural development continuum (adapted, based on IDI research, from the DMIS theory developed by Milton Bennett). Further, the IDI has been demonstrated, through research, to have high predictive validity to both bottom-line cross-cultural outcomes in organizations and intercultural goal accomplishments in education.[2]

---

[2] IDI, "IDI General Information."

The following information provides general information about the IDI as an assessment tool:

> The Intercultural Development Inventory has been psycho-metrically tested and found to possess strong validity and reliability across diverse cultural groups.... This validity includes predictive validity within both the corporate and educational sectors. The IDI has been rigorously tested and has cross-cultural generalizability, both internationally and with domestic diversity. Psychometric scale construction protocols were followed to ensure that the IDI is not culturally biased or susceptible to social desirability effects (i.e., individuals cannot "figure out" how to answer in order to gain a higher score).
>
> The IDI possesses strong content and construct validity. Recent studies also indicate strong predictive validity of the IDI.... In one study within the corporate sector, higher levels of intercultural competence, as measured by the IDI, were strongly predictive of successful recruitment and staffing of diverse talent in organizations. In another study, higher IDI scores among students were predictive of important study abroad outcomes, including greater knowledge of the host culture, less intercultural anxiety when interacting with culturally diverse individuals, increased intercultural friendships, and higher satisfaction with one's study abroad experience.
>
> The IDI is the assessment platform from which IDI Guided Development is undertaken to build intercultural competence based.[3]

To increase in cultural competency, one does not necessarily need to engage directly with the IDI. The ensuing material will explain the various steps needed to begin and progress on the journey toward becoming more culturally competent. Regardless of whether the assessment is taken, the following sections provide actionable steps, directly pulled from the IDI.

---

[3] IDI, "A Valid Assessment Tool."

# Intercultural Development Continuum

Upon completion of the Intercultural Development Inventory (IDI) assessment, the generated results report will designate where an individual will fall regarding his or her intercultural mindset. The intercultural mindset is differentiated between a Monocultural Mindset and an Intercultural Mindset, with Minimization being a transitional Orientation. A Monocultural Mindset emphasizes Denial and Polarization, whereas an Intercultural Mindset will emphasize Acceptance and Adaptation.

While on the surface various individuals may be able to be grouped by similar demographics, but that does not mean that each individual can comprehend and differentiate cultural differences in the same manner. As a result, the IDI charts individual's assessments based on what they term the "Intercultural Development Continuum.[4]

The continuum has five classifications: (1) Denial, (2) Polarization, (3) Minimization, (4) Acceptance, and (5) Adaptation. Following is a detailed explanation of each component of the "Intercultural Development Continuum," as explained in the IDI assessment results.

**Intercultural Development Continuum (IDC™)**

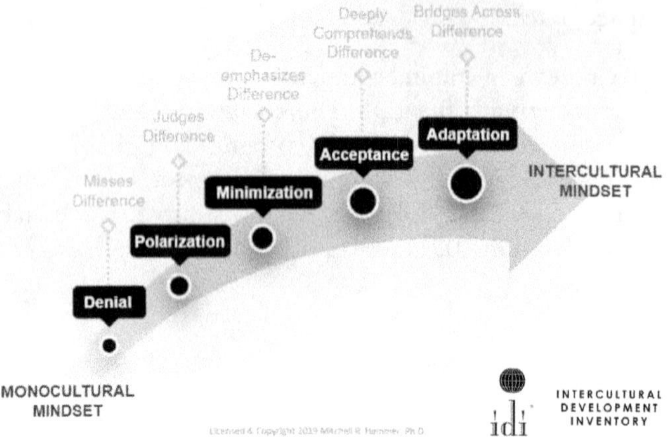


---

[4] The Intercultural Development Continuum will be referred to simply as the continuum.

## Denial

The initial point to address on the continuum is Denial. The IDI provides the following summary of Denial:

> A Denial mindset reflects a more limited capability for understanding and appropriately responding to cultural differences in values, beliefs, perceptions, emotional responses, and behaviors. Denial consists of a Disinterest in other cultures and a more active Avoidance of cultural difference. Individuals with a Denial orientation often do not see differences in perceptions and behavior as "cultural." A Denial orientation is characteristic of individuals who have limited experience with other cultural groups and therefore tend to operate with broad stereotypes and generalizations about the cultural "other." Those at Denial may also maintain a distance from other cultural groups and express little interest in learning about the cultural values and practices of diverse communities. This orientation tends to be associated more with members of a dominant culture as well as members of non-dominant groups who are relatively isolated from mainstream society because both may have more opportunity to remain relatively isolated from cultural diversity. By contrast, members of non-dominant groups who are more actively engaged within the larger, mainstream society are less likely to maintain a Denial orientation, because they more often need to engage cultural differences. When Denial is present in the workplace, cultural diversity oftentimes feels "ignored."[5]

Denial is not the starting point for everyone who wants to become more culturally competent. Instead, Denial could be indicative of someone who intentionally wants to have a monocultural worldview. However, Denial should not be misconstrued as ignorance. Rather, those who are in the Denial category, might choose to be indifferent toward other cultures.

## Polarization

The next point on the continuum is Polarization. The IDI provides the following summary of Polarization:

---

[5] IDI, "IDI General Information: The Intercultural Development Continuum."
https://idiinventory.com/generalinformation/the-intercultural-development-continuum-idc/

Polarization is an evaluative mindset that views cultural differences from an "us versus them" perspective. Polarization can take the form of Defense ("My cultural practices are superior to other cultural practices") or Reversal ("Other cultures are better than mine"). Within Defense, cultural differences are often seen as divisive and threatening to one's own "way of doing things." Reversal is a mindset that values and may idealize other cultural practices while denigrating one's own culture group. Reversal may also support the "cause" of an oppressed group, but this is done with little knowledge of what the "cause" means to people from the oppressed community. When Polarization is present in an organization, diversity typically feels "uncomfortable."[6]

Within popular culture, Polarization could also be understood within the realm of ethnocentrism. One of the characteristics of Polarization is the superiority mindset, which that mindset has fueled systemic racism in America. Unfortunately, Polarization tends to be the approach people take when they feel their position in society is being threatened; they become defensive. However, there is another side to Polarization. IDI terms the other side "Reversal."[7] Reversal manifests as a cultural self-loathing, when an individual views other cultures as being better than their own. Reversal could occur when, for instance, a White person wishes they were Black, or vice versa.

*Minimization*

The third level on the continuum is Minimization. The IDI provides the following summary of Minimization:

> Minimization is a transitional mindset between the more Monocultural orientations of Denial and Polarization and the more Intercultural/Global worldviews of Acceptance and Adaptation. Minimization highlights commonalities in both human Similarity (basic needs) and Universalism (universal values and principles) that can mask a deeper understanding of cultural

---

6 IDI, "IDI General Information: The Intercultural Development Continuum."
https://idiinventory.com/generalinformation/the-intercultural-development-continuum-idc/
7 IDI, "IDI General Information: The Intercultural Development Continuum."
https://idiinventory.com/generalinformation/the-intercultural-development-continuum-idc/

differences. Minimization can take one of two forms: (a) the highlighting of commonalities due to limited cultural self-understanding, which is more commonly experienced by dominant group members within a cultural community; or (b) the highlighting of commonalities as a strategy for navigating the values and practices largely determined by the dominant culture group, which is more often experienced by non-dominant group members within a larger cultural community. This latter strategy can have survival value for non-dominant culture members and often takes the form of "go along to get along." When Minimization exists in organizations, diversity often feels "not heard."[8]

From my experience, Polarization and Minimization are the two categories that most individuals, who desire to increase their cultural competency, initially score. Unfortunately, Minimization best manifests through ignorance. While the Minimization individual acknowledges cultural differences, he or she will tend to minimize or limit the broader understanding of said differences. The limitation translates as cultural ignorance. Minimization can be dangerous because the deeper issues related with cultural differences may not be recognized by the majority cultural group, which, in turn, can frustrate the minority cultural group.

*Acceptance*

The fourth level on the continuum is Acceptance. The IDI provides the following summary of Acceptance:

> Acceptance and Adaptation are intercultural/global mind-sets. With an Acceptance orientation, individuals recognize and appreciate patterns of cultural difference and commonality in their own and other cultures. An Acceptance orientation is curious to learn how a cultural pattern of behavior makes sense within different cultural communities. This involves contrastive self-reflection between one's own culturally learned perceptions and behaviors and perceptions and practices of different cultural groups. While curious, individuals with an Acceptance mindset are not fully able to appropriately adapt to cultural difference.

---

[8] IDI, "IDI General Information: The Intercultural Development Continuum." https://idiinventory.com/generalinformation/the-intercultural-development-continuum-idc/

Someone with an Acceptance orientation may be challenged as well to make ethical or moral decisions across cultural groups. While a person within Acceptance embraces a deeper understanding of cultural differences, this can lead to the individual struggling with reconciling behavior in another cultural group that the person considers unethical or immoral from his or her own cultural viewpoint. When Acceptance is present in organizations and educational institutions, diversity feels "understood."[9]

Acceptance is a two-way street. As the IDI description indicates, Acceptance acknowledges and appreciates commonalities and differences between cultural groups. While Acceptance is a step in the right direction, it also has its limitations. For true cultural competency to be achieved, one must wrestle with the cultural dilemmas that are understood in the Acceptance category; To rectify said dilemmas, the person must progress to the adaptation phase.

*Adaptation*

The fifth level on the continuum is Adaptation. The IDI provides the following summary of Adaptation:

An Adaptation orientation consists of both Cognitive Frame-Shifting (shifting one's cultural perspective) and Behavioral Code-Shifting (changing behavior in authentic and culturally appropriate ways). Adaptation enables deep cultural bridging across diverse communities using an increased repertoire of cultural frameworks and practices in navigating cultural commonalities and differences. An Adaptation mindset sees adaptation in performance (behavior). While people with an Adaptation mindset typically focus on learning adaptive strategies, problems can arise when people with Adaptation mindsets express little tolerance toward people who engage diversity from other developmental orientations. This can result in people with Adaptive capabilities being marginalized in their workplace. When

---

[9] IDI, "IDI General Information: The Intercultural Development Continuum." https://idiinventory.com/generalinformation/the-intercultural-development-continuum-idc/

an Adaptation mindset is present in the workplace, diversity feels "valued and involved."[10]

While adaptation may be the goal, the category does present its own shortcomings. Those found in the Adaptation phase can actually become intolerant to those who are not like-minded, thereby continuing to perpetuate a bifurcated approach to differences. Instead, adaptation in its purest form manifests with cultural humility.

---

10 IDI, "IDI General Information: The Intercultural Development Continuum."
https://idiinventory.com/generalinformation/the-intercultural-development-continuum-idc/

## Conclusion

No matter the starting point, the onus resides on the fact that one needs to begin the journey. However, to do so, the traveler must recognize where he or she is on the continuum. One may make the determination independently, although typically speaking, we tend to overestimate our own orientation. Consequently, that is why the IDI incorporates what is known as an orientation gap to measure the difference between our perceived orientation and our actual orientation.

Therefore, to avoid misrepresenting yourself, I recommend engagement directly with the IDI by completing the assessment with a Qualified Administrator (QA). Regardless of whether you take the assessment, the next chapter illustrates the steps one can take to increase in cultural competency.

# 9

# Ten Key Learning Opportunities

The IDI delineates what they term "Ten Key Intercultural Learning Opportunities."[1] To achieve maximum traction, one must engage with all ten opportunities. To only focus on a few stunts potential growth and could even cause a person to stall in the Minimization mindset.

The following learning opportunities could be facilitated on an individual level or corporately. The journey towards cultural competency should not be experienced in isolation, instead a communal approach will only aid in the growth process.

It is important when addressing each learning opportunity that the cultural competency pilgrim embark on the journey with an open mind and heart. One must continuously adopt a receptive posture despite the experiences that will ensue.

## Learning Opportunity #1:
## Training Programs

Training Programs typically become the most approached and accessed learning opportunity. Many churches and denominational organizations have employed various degrees of training programs through the medium of seminars and conferences. This learning opportunity is the easiest to gain access to and facilitate. Although the nature of training programs includes personal involvement, they also involve the least amount of personal engagement beyond an investment of time. However, Training Programs should not be discarded or invalidated.

---

[1] The 10 Key Opportunities are: Training Programs, Workplace Activities, The Arts, Educational Classes, Personal Interactions, Intercultural Journal, Books, Travel, Coaching, and Site Visits.

Training Programs can benefit pastors, leaders, and church communities in a variety of ways. First, they provide an avenue for the dissemination of culturally appropriate information and cultural context. Information is important to combat misconceptions and misinformation.

Second, providing regular opportunities for Training Programs keeps the topic at the forefront of one's mind, fighting against the propensity to forget the information or relegating it to the proverbial backburner.

Third, repetition in learning is key for long-term cognitive retention. A key phenomenon in the formation of long-term memory is the effect of over learning on retention—discovered by Ebbinghaus in 1885: when the initial training period in a task is prolonged even beyond what is necessary for good immediate recall, long-term retention improves.[2] Being exposed to Training Programs where cultural information is repeated allows people to transfer the information from their short-term memory to their long-term memory.

Fourth, although Training Programs could afford an individual with the ability to blend in and not fully engage, the opposite could also prove true. Training Programs place individuals into a setting where others are presumably on the same quest to learn regarding the topic presented. Therefore, the setting provides the opportunity for personal engagement with people who may encourage, and/or assist, a person with their journey.

Fifth, with some level of intentionality, Training Programs can provide engagement with diverse leaders and diverse perspectives.

## Learning Opportunity #2:
## Workplace Activities

Although earlier in the book it was argued that the church is one of the most segregated places, it does not have to be. Pastors and church leadership can incorporate activities within the local church that educate and empower people regarding cultural competency. Depending on the activity, churches can engage with culturally appropriate activities that educate and inform.

Additionally, cultural activities within the church context provide a disruption to the "business as usual" effect that can occur within a work environment. Bringing activities into the church environment assists with the church becoming an ally with communities who feel underrepresented

---

[2] Joiner and Smith. "Long-Term Retention Explained," 2948-2955.

or misunderstood. Being an ally "means someone who is not being directly harmed by the injustice in question yet who stands with those being harmed, even if it's against the self-interest of their identity privilege."[3] Therefore, by bringing the activity into the church, the action provides a demonstration of advocacy and empathy on the part of the church leadership. Additionally, the action serves as an example to the parishioners; demonstrating an action to be emulated.

## Learning Opportunity #3:
## Theatre, Film, and Arts

The term *culture* "refers to the body of knowledge and manners acquired by an individual, while the second describes the shared customs, values and beliefs which characterize a given social group, and which are passed down from generation to generation."[4] Many cultural customs, values, and beliefs manifest through theatre, film, and arts. Therefore, utilizing those modalities as a means of cultural competency growth provides the learner with the opportunity to engage with cultural nuances in a new way.

The arts manifested through theatre, film, and other artistic expressions can provide the cultural competency learner opportunity to experience the cultural distinctives of other ethnic and racial groups. Although one might deem artistic expression as unimportant or even pedantic, it provides an in-depth look into aspects of ethnic and racial culture perhaps not effectively articulated through verbal expression. With this learning opportunity, it is important not to relegate the experiences to only one modality and/or one experience. To truly advance in cultural competency, one needs to engage with all styles continuously.

## Learning Opportunity #4:
## Educational Classes

Prior to the advent of the Internet Age, this learning opportunity proved to be difficult. Geography presented a barrier that limited individuals' access to educational classes, particularly if a person lived in a community far from a metro area or college/university. While many colleges and universities have offered educational classes related to other ethnic groups or sociological classes for decades, such courses were only

---

3 Kendi and Blain, *Four Hundred Souls*, 62.
4 Gindro, "Culture."

accessible to those physically able to travel to the campus whereas today, most colleges and universities have embraced some form of digital education making courses available to the masses.

Educational classes have not been entrusted solely to the college system. Recent digital advances have created unprecedented access to educational classes through new modalities. A few sources to consider, including some pros and cons, follows:

- **TED Talks.** This format has become normative in the modern society. Ted Talks manifest as brief monologues that provide rich content within a short time frame.
  - o Pro – Speakers have been vetted and deemed experts in their field.
  - o Con – The shorter content may not provide enough context to satisfy the topic.
- **YouTube videos.** This platform provides a vast array of content and perspectives.
  - o Pro – This venue has an extremely large amount of content, which includes extensive content and not only short snippets.
  - o Con – Sources have not been vetted. Therefore, content could be extremely opinionated and/or invalid.
- **Social Media.** Social Media has progressed since the early '90s when it manifested as "chat rooms" and "instant messenger." Currently, modern social media platforms have morphed into life-altering, culture shaping entities.
  - o Pro – Social media venues are widely utilized by an ample percentage of the society, thus providing easy access of viewing as an individual or a community.
  - o Con – Content can be extremely polarizing and opinionated. Additionally, algorithms used by social media companies can customize content to align with the user's preferences, which could in turn limit the person's exposure to differing perspectives.
- **Community Based Educational Classes.** Many cities and neighborhoods increasingly offer community-based classes geared toward ethnic and cultural engagement and enrichment.
  - o Pro – Such classes provide direct engagement with other cultures and ethnic groups and ongoing opportunities for direct interaction, which can produce friendships and connections.

    o   Con – Access could be limited because of proximity or availability of the individual.

The above list is only a sample of educational class opportunities outside of the college/university setting. Individuals should be encouraged to seek out other educational classes unique to their own community.

# Learning Opportunity #5:
## Personal Interactions

I cannot emphasize enough the importance of this learning opportunity. One's ability to directly and personally interact with other cultures and ethnic groups presents one of the best, perhaps the greatest, avenue toward increasing cultural competency. By seeking out personal interactions, the individual chooses to step outside of his or her world and into someone else's. Although this learning opportunity is the most ideal, it has limitations.

When engaging in conversations with people who desire to increase in cultural competency, many ask some form of the question: Do I just need to become friends with a black person? While the answer to this question is "Yes," the question itself lends to a myopic approach.

One of the fallacies encountered when engaging in conversations related to race and culture is confusing one person's experiences as normative for everyone within that person's racial, ethnic, or cultural group. These skewed conclusions manifest as stereotypes, which could be indicative of some people but never include everyone—thus reinforcing biases and racist ideologies.

The pursuit of personal interactions should not become static but constantly stay at the forefront of the pursuer's endeavors. The individual should look for a multitude of personal interaction connecting points, which will in turn assist in diversifying their learning opportunity, enriching the experience.

# Learning Opportunity #6:
## Books and Articles

The natural propensity is for a person to gravitate toward scenarios that provide safety, security, and a certain measure of comfort. Engaging different cultures can create anxiety, which could inadvertently steer the individual toward more comfortable or natural resources. When choosing books and articles to read, it is easy to gravitate toward similar ideologies and vantage points. This remains true not only of ethnic, cultural, and racial groups but also with respect to gender. Because individuals tend to lean toward similar perspectives, they often read books and/or articles related to perspectives they agree with, or perspectives originating from a demographic like their own because that feels natural and comfortable and presents the least resistance. Therefore, individuals should employ ongoing effort to engage with diverse voices in print.

When selecting books and articles to read, seek out perspectives from diverse writers. Unfortunately, diverse authors in some arenas may not be prevalent, which means that the individual may need to do some research to engage with diverse authors. The objective with this learning opportunity does not mean that a person could not read materials written by someone from their own demographic, but that the person needs to intentionally include diverse voices on the topic.

A good example to illustrate this point: In my current role at North Central University, I teach the class, "Reading and Interpreting Scripture." When I realized that the voices I was using were all white males, I began to seek out resources from other perspectives and discovered the book, *Reading While Black: African American Biblical Interpretation as an Exercise in Hope* by Esau McCaulley. After reading the book, it transformed the way I teach and garnered recognition from the various diverse student groups in my class.

# Learning Opportunity #7:
## Intercultural Journal

Self-awareness is one of the primary keys to cultural competency. Keeping an intercultural journal presents an excellent opportunity to become more self-aware with regard to how you personally perceive, value, and interact with people different from your own cultural group. The intercultural journal could present itself in two ways.

- First, the journal could be a means of observing and reflecting on cultural differences and commonalities that you might observe throughout the day—perhaps about other people's interactions or observations about your own interactions. Through these observations, you can take note of how people perceive, value, and act in ways similar to or different from your own cultural group.

- Second, the journal could focus on observations related to what the IDI terms "critical incidents"—observed interactions where cultural differences emerge. In these interactions, you will want to observe whether the people involved recognized the cultural differences and if they respond appropriately. The IDI recommends recording the following elements: who was involved, what happened, what you think were the cultural differences present, how people responded, and the outcome.

This learning opportunity can provide an excellent informative space for the individual but does present a challenge. If the individual making the observations is not personally aware of his or her own cultural biases, that person could inadvertently misinterpret whether the differences observed are appropriate or not. Despite the stated challenge, the learning opportunity still remains a viable tool.

Once the observer becomes more self-aware, they will have a journal full of observed interactions to go back to for reexamining the previous interactions. Looking at the interactions through a new self-aware lens could provide a catalytic moment for the individual. Additionally, the journal could lead to the individual recognizing their own cultural biases, or finally recognize a situation where inequity occurred.

## Learning Opportunity #8:
## Travel

The learning opportunity of travel can manifest in a multitude of ways. An article published by the *New York Post* found that only 11 percent of people travel outside their state. Even more surprising is that 54 percent said they have only visited ten states or less.[5] Therefore, simply choosing to travel within your country can provide an excellent cultural learning opportunity. Within the United States, one can experience so many cultural opportunities. Traveling to different states and different geographical regions exposes the individual to the various cultural nuances that exist.

International travel presents a whole new cultural learning opportunity. Unfortunately, almost half (46 percent) of Americans have never traveled to more than one international country.[6] Traveling internationally provides the individual with the opportunity to view how other cultures interact, make decisions, share information, and treat tourists. This perspective allows the observer to reflect on how they might treat tourists who visit their community.

---

5 Schmall, "A Shocking Number of Americans Never Leave Home."
6 Silver, "Most Americans Have Traveled Abroad."

To maximize this learning opportunity, one must seek to systematically observe and engage with cultural diversity. When traveling outside of one's home region, it could be easy to remain isolated. Intentionality must be employed by the onlooker to ensure the experience is efficiently augmented.

## Learning Opportunity #9:
## Site Visits

Building on Learning Opportunity #8 is the idea of seeking out site visit locations. There are well known site visit locations like Ellis Island or the National Civil Rights Museum. Site visits might require some level of research, or they might be something one simply stumbles upon. For instance, one time while visiting New Orleans, I discovered the "Whitney Plantation" tour. For the next hour, I learned so much about the history of slavery and the experience of slaves on plantations.

The goal with site visits is to seek out opportunities where you can increase your knowledge about diverse cultural experiences. Museums are good options, but you will want to ensure that the museum provides varied cultural encounters. These experiences could be enhanced if you make the effort to engage with someone who can share some additional cultural expertise for you to gain a deeper understanding to maximize the site visit.

## Learning Opportunity #10:
## Intercultural Coaching

Those who desire to take the experience to another level can engage with intercultural coaching. The method I would recommend is the one I utilized, based on the IDI. I loved the experience and gleaned so much as a result of the IDI that I took it to another level and became a Qualified Administrator of the IDI. However, the IDI is not the only option.

The other resource I would recommend is *Cultural Intelligence* by David Livermore. The Cultural Intelligence Center provides the student with what they term a "CQ Profile." The profile allows the participant to better understand where they rate in various categories compared to others throughout the world.

Other coaching opportunities exist, but the two mentioned above are ones I have personally vetted and deem of high quality and beneficial for the individual.

# Conclusion

Reading through the list of learning opportunities can feel overwhelming or daunting. In reality it *is* overwhelming and daunting. The process of increasing cultural competency is not an easy—or neat—process; nor does it occur in one day or one week. Increasing cultural competency requires dedication, commitment, and time. While the Learning Opportunities are the medium utilized to facilitate the process of increasing one's cultural competency, one component should not be overlooked.

I am an avid user of social media with Facebook being my typical "go-to" app. One of the main reasons I check Facebook daily is because of the Memories feature. I love looking back at past events and experiences. I love seeing how much my children have grown throughout the years. I love reflecting on friendships that have emerged over time. Likewise, in the journey of cultural competency, each person needs a way to document and memorialize their experience with the intent to review and reflect on later. Therefore, it is my recommendation that you find a way to journal the process. Although the effect of these journals cannot be substantiated statistically, they provided a means for the participants to process their experiences. The introspective, reflective aspect of the process proves vital.

---

Cultural competency comes through experience,
which leads to revelation.

---

Cultural competency is not obtained by merely completing a series of steps; rather, it comes through experience, which leads to revelation. The experiences are designed to guide an individual toward their catalytic event. The catalytic event can occur as the direct result of an experience or through the internal processing that occurs later; such events provide a way for each participant to document their own internal processing. If you willingly engage with the process, the results will be palatable and the impact exponential.

# 10

# Moving Forward

It is my impression that church leadership and congregants are embracing a shift towards diversity and integration. Although the endeavor should be applauded and celebrated, it is important to understand that without cultural competency training, diversity integration becomes a fleeting effort. Once the cultural competency journey has commenced the impending results will manifest fruit that remains.

The Church is in a unique position to be the frontrunner in the area of cultural competency. By implementing the aforementioned process both at the local church and denominational levels, it can systematically prepare current and future ministers to be more culturally competent. These leaders would serve as examples by identifying their neighbor while also taking the steps necessary to engage their neighbor, just as Jesus illustrated in the story of the Good Samaritan.

## Practical Impact

A year removed from the project of guiding students through the Learning Opportunities, conversations I had with the participants all confirmed that the project had impacted them exponentially. Even the participants who initially appeared to not make significant progress reported that they are now more aware of cultural differences, in addition to being more cognizant of their actions and mindset toward differing cultures. The informal progress from participants over the course of a year indicates substantiation of the learning opportunities effectiveness. As current and future ministers receive training in cultural competency, the ripple effect's impact increases proportionately.

Annually, the AG releases data reporting church growth within the Fellowship. While traditionally a predominately White denomination, the recent data for the AG shows the largest increase has occurred among minorities, specifically African Americans and Hispanics.[1] Cities across America are becoming more and more diverse, even smaller towns. Therefore, there is increased merit to the process of engaging Learning

---

[1] Assemblies of God, "Statistics."

Opportunities. In so doing, it will help pastors gain confidence in understanding different cultural groups. With understanding, the pastor will feel better equipped to engage the other cultural groups, by strategically structuring their ministry enterprises to incorporate culturally competent initiatives. In doing so, the pastor can effectively mobilize and cultivate diversity within their communities. As ministers embrace an ethos of cultural competency, their influence will multiple, which in turn will serve as a catalyst for other churches to come alongside and learn from their example.

For ministers to adjust to the shifts in ethnic diversity, current and future pastors need to embrace a culturally competent approach to ministry in ethnically diverse populations. Therefore, cultural competency training within local pastors and church leadership seems like a logical starting point.

Additionally, if Christian colleges and universities would incorporate cultural competency training within their degree programs, it would allow future vocational ministers to enter the workforce, not only equipped to minister but also equipped for effective cross-cultural ministry. By embracing cultural competency training, denominations can take a proactive stance regarding the demographic shift among their constituency.

By combining ministerial training for effective cross-cultural ministry with local churches intent to engage the process, the result has the potential to see the local church become a leader in racial reconciliation. While individual growth regarding cultural competency is important and necessary, racism needs to be addressed on a larger platform. Due to the systemic nature of racism, larger systems need to address the bifurcation of races in America. Churches and denominations could use this process as an initial road map by which to corporately help ministers increase their cultural competence.

Individuals embracing a path toward cultural competency is needed, but for true change to occur, larger systems, like the church, and not just my own denomination, need to intentionally make steps toward integrating cultural competency training.

## Recommendations for Future Study

The impetus of this process focused on increasing the cultural competency of Caucasian-Americans as related to African Americans. Therefore, the research for this process incorporated research on African American history as well as the construct of racism. However, both areas of study need further research. This book did not focus specifically on racism and African American history but merely incorporated components of both. I quickly realized that racism is a much deeper and broader subject as is African American history. Couple racism with racial prejudice and the rabbit trails became numerous. During the research process, I often faced the temptation of pursuing those rabbit trails. However, I resisted the temptation by keeping a list of resources for future investigation.

Research for this book made me aware that I have only begun to scratch the surface of African American history. Following the experience encountered during my research, I realized that there is so much more that needs to be uncovered, understood, and appreciated. The richness of Black history has been overshadowed by the systems that have tried to bury the past. However, people need to acquire a fuller comprehension of African American history in totality—which includes the good, the bad, and the ugly. Further research into African American history requires further exploration and unearthing. After the Glossary, I have included my Bibliography, which includes the works cited in the book in addition to resources which could be used for further study. Although the list is extensive, it is my hope that the content will provide you with a starting point for our own journey.

An additional area for further research should focus on defining racism. Depending on the audience, the word carries many preconceived notions and elicits varying responses. An understanding of African American history requires an understanding and definition of racism. Unfortunately, people cannot agree on a definition for racism, which raises a larger issue. If racism cannot be defined and understood, how can we come to a consensus on how to deal with the problem?

For instance, there is a lack of consensus as to what term is most appropriate when referring to African Americans. Some sources opted for African American, which seems to be the more politically correct term, whereas other sources utilized the more ambiguous term of Black. Ironically, I noticed more African Americans used the term Black while Caucasian-Americans tended to use the term African American. This differentiation needs further exploration, particularly because the term Black was created and utilized as a result of the slave trade. The roots of the term are steeped in a racist history and only exacerbate the racial bifurcation in America.

Because this book focused on cultural competency related to African Americans, further study regarding other American minority groups would be beneficial to the development of cultural competency.

Depending on the demographic make-up of a community, a pastor will need to adjust the area of study to coincide with the ethnic groups present in his or her area. However, the steps required for increased cultural competency do not change. Since the Hispanic population has grown larger than the African American population,[2] further study needs to focus on the various Hispanic people groups.

---

[2] U.S. Census Bureau, "Quick Facts."

# Conclusion to Part Three

At the outset of this book, I felt confident in my experiences and knowledge regarding African American culture. Years later, I have progressed beyond seeking cultural competency to embracing cultural humility. The more I learn, the more I realize that I have so much more to grasp. The quest for cultural competency should never culminate with a feeling of completion, but rather lead one toward a deeper appreciation of the differences present in other people, as well as the differences present within oneself. These differences shouldn't be feared or ignored but instead should be acknowledged, explored, and embraced.

More than ever, this book convinced me of the deep need for cultural competency training. Individual advancement in cultural competency is a step in the right direction, but strategic organizational intentionality that focuses on crossing the racial divide will produce immediate change as well as change for generations to come. By implementing various aspect of this book into one's personal context, any individual could experience an increase in cultural competence. However, one must give special attention to the utilization of an assessment tool as a means of evaluating and appraising one's progress. These assessment tools will provide understanding into a person's self-awareness in terms of other cultural groups as well as into his or her own culture. Utilizing the tools, with an open heart and an awareness of the Holy Spirit, any current pastor or future pastor could move toward being more effective in reaching diverse populations in local communities.

# Glossary

*African American.* An American who is of Black African descent.

*black.* For the sake of this book, the descriptive term of "black" will be used when applied to a single person, or when used as a designator.

*Black.* For the sake of this book, the term "Black" will be used, correspondently with African American, when addressing specific ethnic and cultural traits, or when used as a designator of a group or ideology. Within the research, there was not a clear consensus regarding what term would be deemed more appropriate. Some sources preferred Black over African American and vice versa; therefore, the terms will be used interchangeably.

*Caucasian or Caucasian-American.* An American who is of English or White European descent.

*Cultural Competency.* The knowledge that enables people to understand and appropriately interact with a culture different from their own.

*Culture.* The customs, beliefs, social norms, and material traits of an ethnic group.

*IDI.* Intercultural Development Inventory.

*Ministry.* For the sake of this project, the term ministry will be applied to vocational church ministry.

*Prejudice.* A preconceived judgment or opinion usually based on limited information.

*Racism.* Culturally acceptable beliefs that defend social advantages based on race.

*Racist.* A person who shows or feels discrimination or prejudice against people of other races.

*Twin Cities.* Refers to the metropolitan area of Minneapolis and St. Paul, Minnesota.

*white.* For the sake of this book, the descriptive term of "White" will be used when applied to a single person.

*White.* For the sake of this book, the term "White" will be used, interchangeably with Caucasian-American, when addressing specific ethnic and cultural traits, or when used as a designator of a group or ideology.

# Bibliography and Additional Resources

"Celebrating African American Culture & History." Huntsville-Madison County Public Library. Updated January 24, 2018. Accessed October 15, 2018. https://guides.hmcpl.org/AfricanAmericanHistory.

"New Census Bureau Report Analyzes U.S. Population Projections." Accessed July 27, 2016. http://www.census.gov/newsroom/press-releases/2015/cb15-tps16.html.

"Population Estimates, July 1, 2015, (V2015)." Minneapolis City Minnesota QuickFacts from the US Census Bureau. Accessed July 27, 2016. https://www.census.gov/quickfacts/table/PST045215/2743000,00#flag-js-X.

"Somali Community in US: Demographics." Somali Community in US: Demographics. Accessed July 27, 2016. http://www.allied-media.com/Somali_American/Somali_American_demographics.html.

"Your Geography Selections." American FactFinder. Accessed July 27, 2016. http://factfinder.census.gov/faces/tableservices/jsf/pages/productview.xhtml?src=bkmk.

Alexander, Estrelda Y. *Black Fire: One Hundred Years of African American Pentecostalism.* Downers Grove, IL: IVP Academic, 2011.

Alexander, Estrelda, and Albert George Miller. *The Black Fire Reader: A Documentary Resource on African American Pentecostalism.* Eugene, OR: Cascade Books, 2013.

Alexander, Michelle. *The New Jim Crow Mass Incarceration in the Age of Colorblindness.* New York, NY: New Press, 2012.

Allen, Theodore. *The Invention of the White Race: Racial Oppression and Social Control.* Vol. 1. London, England: Verso, 2012.

Althouse, Peter. "Contributions of Christology to the Theology of Godly Love." In *The Science and Theology of Godly Love*, edited by Matthew T. Lee and Amos Yong, 56-76. DeKalb, IL: Northern Illinois University Press, 2012.

Alvaro L. Nieves, and Robert J. Priest. *This Side of Heaven: Race, Ethnicity, and Christian Faith.* Oxford, England: Oxford University Press, 2007.

Aquinas, Thomas. *Summa Theologica.* Notre Dame, IN: Christian Classics, 1948.

Arland J. Hultgren. "Enlarging the Neighborhood: The Parable of the Good Samaritan (Luke 10:25-37)." *Word & World* 37, no. 1 (2017): 71-78.

Assemblies of God. "AG USA Adherents by Race." AG.org, accessed
        September 18, 2018. https://ag.org/-
        /media/AGORG/Downloads/Statistics/Attendance-and-
        Adherents/2017-Adherents-by-Race.pdf
Augustine. The *Fathers of the Church*. Washington, DC: The Catholic University of
        America, 1991.
Bailey, Kenneth E. *Jesus through Middle Eastern Eyes: Cultural Studies in the Gospels*.
        Downers Grove, IL: IVP Academic, 2008.
————. *The Cross & the Prodigal: Luke 15 through the Eyes of Middle Eastern Peasants*.
        Downers Grove, IL: InterVarsity Press, 2005.
Barna Group. *Barna Trends 2017: What's New and What's next at the Intersection of
        Faith and Culture*. Grand Rapids, MI: Baker Books, 2016.
————. *Barna Trends 2018: What's New and What's next at the Intersection of Faith
        and Culture*. Grand Rapids, MI: Baker Books, 2017.
Barth, Karl. *Church Dogmatics*. Louisville, KY: Westminster John Knox Press,
        1994.
Berlejung, Angelika. *Die Theologie der Bilder: Herstellung und Einweihung von
        Kultbildern in Mesopotamien unddie alttestamentliche Bilderpolemik* [The
        Theology of Images: Production and Inauguration of Cult Images in
        Mesopotamia and the Old Testament Image Polemics]. Fribourg,
        Germany: Vandenhoeck & Ruprecht, 1998.
Block, Daniel Isaac. *Judges, Ruth*. Nashville, TN: Broadman & Holman, 1999.
Borchert, Gerald L. *John 1-11*. Vol. 25A of *The New American Commentary*.
        Nashville, TN: Broadman & Holman, 1996.
Boyd, Greg. "Racism: Why Whites have Trouble 'Getting It.'" ReKnew.org.
        Accessed November 16, 2018.
Brand, Chad. s.v. "Mixed Multitude." In *Holman Illustrated Bible Dictionary*, edited
        by Chad Brand, Charles Draper, Archie England, Steve Bond, E. Ray
        Clendenen, and Trent C. Butler, 1145. Nashville, TN: Holman Bible
        Publishers, 2003.
Breckenridge, James F., and Lillian Breckenridge. *What Color is Your God?:
        Multicultural Education in the Church*. Grand Rapids, MI: Baker Books,
        2003.
Breneman, Mervin. *Ezra, Nehemiah, Esther*. Vol. 10 of *The New American
        Commentary*. Nashville, TN: Broadman and Holman, 1993.
Brooks, Clem, and Jeff Manza. "Social Cleavages and Political Alignments: U.S.
        Presidential Elections, 1960 to 1992." *American Sociological Review* 62, no.
        6 (1997): 937-946.
Brooks, Clem, and Jeff Manza. "Social Cleavages and Political Alignments: U.S.
        Presidential Elections, 1960 to 1992." *American Sociological Review* 62, no.
        6 (1997): 937-946.
Brown, Donald E. *Human Universals*. New York, NY: McGraw-Hill, 1991.
Bruce, F. F. *The Book of Acts*. Grand Rapids, MI: Eerdmans, 1988.
Brueggemann, Walter. *Genesis*. Louisville, KY: Westminster John Knox, 2010.

Bultmann, Rudolf. *History of the Synoptic Tradition*. New York, NY: Harper & Row, 1968.

Calvin, John. *Institutes of the Christian Religion*. Louisville, KY: Westminster John Knox, 2006.

Carson, Donald Arthur. *The Gospel According to John*. Grand Rapids: Eerdmans, 2016.

Churchill, Winston. Optimize.me. Accessed October 21, 2018, https://www.optimize.me/ quotes/winston-churchill/307042-there-comes-a-certain-moment-in-everyones-life-a-moment/.

Cleveland, Christena. *Disunity in Christ: Uncovering the Hidden Forces that Keep Us Apart*. Downers Grove, IL: IVP Books, 2013.

CNN Library. "Trayvon Martin Shooting Fast Facts." Updated May 7, 2018. Accessed November 2, 2018 https://www.cnn.com/2013/06/05/us/trayvon-martin-shooting-fast-facts/index.html.

Cortez, Marc. *Christological Anthropology in Historical Perspective: Ancient and Contemporary Approaches to Theological Anthropology*. Grand Rapids, MI: Zondervan, 2016.

Craigie, Peter C. *The Book of Deuteronomy*. Grand Rapids, MI: Eerdmans, 2007.

Denevi, Elizabeth. "What if Being Called Racist is the Beginning, not the End, of the Conversation?" In *The Guide for White Women Who Teach Black Boys*, edited by Eddie Moore Jr, Ali Michael, and Marguerite W. Penick-Parks, 74-78. Thousand Oaks, CA: Corwin Publishing, 2018.

DeYmaz, Mark, and Harry Li. *Leading a Healthy Multi-Ethnic Church*. Grand Rapids, MI: Zondervan, 2010.

DeYmaz, Mark, and Oneya Fennell Okuwobi. *Multiethnic Conversations: An Eight-Week Journey Toward Unity in Your Church*. Indianapolis, IN: Wesleyan Publishing House, 2016.

DiAngelo, Robin, and Michael Eric Dyson. *White Fragility Why It's So Hard for White People to Talk about Racism*. Boston, MA: Beacon Press, 2018.

Douglas, Mary. *The Active Voice*. New York, NY: Routledge, 1982.

Dubois, David L., and Michael J. Karcher. *Handbook of Youth Mentoring*. Thousand Oaks, CA: SAGE Publications, 2013.

Dyer, Richard. *White: Twentieth Anniversary Edition*. New York, NY: Routledge, 2017.

Easton, M. G. "Samaritans." In *Easton's Bible Dictionary*, edited by M. G. Easton. New York, NY: Harper & Brothers, 1893. Logos.

Edersheim, Alfred. *The Bible History, Old Testament*. Peabody, MA: Hendrickson, 1995.

Edgar, William. *Created and Creating: A Biblical Theology of Culture*. Downers Grove, IL: IVP Academic, 2016.

Edwards, James R. *The Gospel According to Luke*. Grand Rapids, MI: Eerdmans, 2015.

Elmore, Tim. *Generation IY: Our Last Chance to save Their Future*. Atlanta, GA: Poet Gardener Publishing, 2010.

Elwell Walter A., and Barry J. Beitzel. "Elohim." In *Baker Encyclopedia of the Bible*, edited by Walter A. Elwell and Barry J. Beitzel, 697. Grand Rapids, MI: Baker Book House, 1988.

———. "Foreigner." In *Baker Encyclopedia of the Bible*, edited by Walter A. Elwell and Barry J. Beitzel, 806-807. Grand Rapids, MI: Baker Book House, 1988.

———. "Samaritans." In *Baker Encyclopedia of the Bible*, edited by Walter A. Elwell and Barry J. Beitzel, 1886-1888. Grand Rapids, MI: Baker Book House, 1988.

Emerson, Michael O., and Christian Smith. *Divided by Faith: Evangelical Religion and the Problem of Race in America*. New York, NY: Oxford Press, 2000

Emerson, Michael, and George Yancey. *Transcending Racial Barriers: Toward a Mutual Obligations Approach*. New York, NY: Oxford Press, 2011.

Enns, Peter. *Exodus: NIV Application Commentary: From Biblical Text to Contemporary Life*. Grand Rapids, MI: Zondervan, 2000.

Erickson, Millard. *Christian Theology*. Grand Rapids, MI: Baker, 1998.

Esler, Philip E. "Jesus and the Reduction of Intergroup Conflict: The Parable of the Good Samaritan in the Light of Social Identity Theory." *BibInt* 8 (2000): 325-357.

Evans, Mary J. *Judges and Ruth: An Introduction and Commentary*. Downers Grove, IL: IVP Academic, 2017.

Ewing, W. "Samaritans." In *The International Standard Bible Encyclopaedia*, edited by James Orr, John L. Nuelsen, Edgar Y. Mullins, and Morris O. Evans, 2673-2674. Chicago, IL: The Howard-Severance Company, 1915.

Farina, Salvatore E. "Leadership Development Coaching: Best Practices for Improving Performance in Crafting Vision, Building Alignment, and Championing Implementation." DMin. proj., Assemblies of God Theological Seminary, 2015.

Fensham, Frank Charles. *The Books of Ezra and Nehemiah*. Grand Rapids, MI: Eerdmans, 2007.

Flynn, Andrea, Susan Holmberg, Felicia J. Wong, and Dorian Tod Warren. *The Hidden Rules of Race: Barriers to an Inclusive Economy*. New York, NY: Cambridge University Press, 2018.

Funk, Robert. *Language, Hermeneutic, and Word of God*. New York, NY: Harper and Row, 1966.

Gaebelein Frank E., and Dick Polcyn. *Deuteronomy - 2 Samuel*. Vol. 3 of *The Expositor's Bible Commentary: With the New International Version of the Holy Bible*. Grand Rapids, MI: Zondervan, 1992.

Gane, Roy E. *Leviticus, Numbers*. Grand Rapids, MI: Zondervan, 2004.

Gangel, Kenneth O. *Acts*. Vol. 5 of *Holman New Testament Commentary*. Nashville, TN: Broadman & Holman Publishers, 1998.

Garland, David E. *Luke*. Grand Rapids, MI: Zondervan, 2012.

Garrett, Duane A. *A Commentary on Exodus*. Grand Rapids, MI: Kregel
 Academic, 2014.

Gilliard, Dominique DuBois. *Rethinking Incarceration: Advocating for Justice that
 Restores*. Downers Grove, IL: InterVarsity Press, 2018.

Glazer, Nathan. "America's Ethnic Pattern, 'Melting Pot' or 'Nation of
 Nations'?" *Commentary* 15 (January 1953): 401-408.

Green, Joel B. *The Gospel of Luke*. Grand Rapids, MI: Eerdmans, 1997.

Grenz, Stanley. *The Social God and the Relational Self*. Louisville, KY: Westminster
 John Knox Press, 2001.

Hamilton, Victor P. *The Book of Genesis: Chapters 1-17*. Grand Rapids, MI:
 Eerdmans, 1990.

————. *The Book of Genesis: Chapters 18-50*. Grand Rapids, MI: Eerdmans, 1995.

Harrington, Daniel. *The Maccabean Revolt: Anatomy of a Biblical Revolution*. Eugene,
 OR: Wipf and Stock, 2009.

Hess, Richard S. "Equality with and without Innocence." In *Discovering Biblical
 Equality: Complementarity without Hierarchy*, 2nd ed., edited by Ronald W.
 Pierce, Rebecca Merrill Groothius, Gordon D. Fee, 79-95. Downers
 Grove, IL: IVP Academic, 2005.

Hill, Daniel. *White Awake: An Honest Look at What It Means to Be White*. Downers
 Grove, IL: InterVarsity Press, 2017.

Hook, Joshua N., and Don Davis, *Cultural Humility: Engaging Diverse Identity in
 Therapy*. Washington, DC: American Psychological Association, 2017.

Hook, Joshua N., Don E. Davis, Jesse Owen, Everett L. Worthington Jr., and
 Shawn O. Utsey. "Cultural Humility: Measuring Openness to Culturally
 Diverse Clients." *Journal of Counseling Psychology* 60, no. 3 (2013): 353-
 366.

Hopkins, Dwight N. *Down, Up, and Over: Slave Religion and Black Theology*.
 Minneapolis, MN: Fortress Press, 2000.

Hubbard, Robert L. *The Book of Ruth*. Grand Rapids, MI: Eerdmans, 2007.

Intercultural Development Inventory. "The Roadmap to Intercultural
 Competency Using the IDI," accessed October 2, 2018,
 https://idiinventory.com/publications/.

Irenaeus. *Proof of the Apostolic Preaching*. New York, NY: MacMillan Company,
 1920. Kindle.

Jefferson Thomas, et al. *The Declaration of Independence* 1776.

Johnson, Jerry A. "Image of God." In *Holman Illustrated Bible Dictionary*, edited by
 Chad Brand, Charles Draper, Archie England, Steve Bond, E. Ray
 Clendenen, Trent C. Butler, and Bill Latta, 806-807. Nashville, TN:
 Holman Bible Publishers, 2003.

Josephus, Flavius. *The Works of Josephus: Complete and Unabridged in One Volume*.
 Peabody, MA: Hendrickson, 1987.

Keil, C. F., and F. Delitzsch. *The Pentateuch*. Vol. 1 of *Commentary on the Old
 Testament*. Peabody, MA: Hendrickson, 1996.

Kendi, Ibram X. *Stamped from the Beginning: The Definitive History of Racist Ideas in America*. New York, NY: Nation Books, 2016.

Klink, Edward W. *John: Zondervan Exegetical Commentary on the New Testament*. Grand Rapids, MI: Zondervan, 2016.

Kostenberger, Andreas J. *Baker Exegetical Commentary on the New Testament: John*. Grand Rapids, MI: Baker Academic, 2004.

Kruse, Colin G. *Paul's Letter to the Romans*. Grand Rapids, MI: Eerdmans, 2012.

Kugel, James L. *The Bible as It Was*. Cambridge, MA: Harvard Press, 1997.

Landsman, Julie. "The State of the White Woman Teacher." In *The Guide For White Women Who Teach Black Boys*, edited by Eddie Moore Jr, Ali Michael, and Marguerite W. Penick-Parks, 28-39. Thousand Oaks, CA: Corwin Publishing, 2018.

Lee, Matthew T., and Amos Yong. *The Science and Theology of Godly Love*. Dekalb, IL: Northern Illinois University Press, 2012.

Lingenfelter, Sherwood. *Agents of Transformation: A Guide for Effective Cross-Cultural Ministry*. Grand Rapids, MI: Baker, 1996.

Lingenfelter, Judith, and Sherwood G. Lingenfelter. *Teaching Cross-culturally: An Incarnational Model for Learning and Teaching*. Grand Rapids, MI: Baker Academic, 2004.

————. *Leading Cross-culturally: Covenant Relationships for Effective Christian Leadership*. Grand Rapids, MI: Baker Academic, 2009.

Lingenfelter, Sherwood G., and Marvin K. Mayers. *Ministering Cross-culturally: A Model for Effective Personal Relationships*. Grand Rapids, MI: Baker Academic, 2016.

Livermore, David A. *Cultural Intelligence: Improving Your CQ to Engage Our Multicultural World*. Grand Rapids, MI: Baker Academic, 2009.

————. *Leading with Cultural Intelligence: The Real Secret to Success*. New York: Amacom, 2015.

Longenecker, Richard N. *Galatians*. Grand Rapids, MI: Zondervan, 2015.

Loritts, Bryan C. *Right Color, Wrong Culture: The Type of Leader Every Organization Needs to Become Multi-ethnic*. Chicago, IL: Moody Publishers, 2014.

Loury, Glenn C. *One by One from the Inside Out: Essays and Reviews on Race and Responsibility in America*. New York, NY: Free Press, 1995.

Manser, Martin H. *Dictionary of Bible Themes: The Accessible and Comprehensive Tool for Topical Studies*. London, England: Martin Manser, 2009. Logos.

Martin Luther King, Jr. Interview on "Meet the Press." April 17, 1960. Accessed October 14, 2018. https://www.youtube.com/watch?v=1q881g1L_d8.

Matthews, Kenneth A. *Genesis 1-11:26*. Vol. 1a of *The New American Commentary*. Nashville, TN: Broadman and Holdman, 1996.

Mattson, Stephen. "Social Justice is a Christian Tradition-Not a Liberal Agenda," https://sojo.net/articles/social-justice-christian-tradition-not-liberal-agenda. Accessed October 17, 2018.

McCall, Leslie. *The Undeserving Rich*. New York, NY: Cambridge Press, 2013.

McDonald, Dee. "Preview Day Introduction." Address, North Central University Preview Day. Minneapolis, MN. June 17, 2016.

McDonald, J. I. H. "The View from the Ditch—and Other Angles: Interpreting the Parable of the Good Samaritan." *Scottish Journal of Theology 49* (1996): 21-37.

McDonald, Jason. *American Ethnic History: Themes and Perspectives*. Edinburgh, England: Edinburgh University Press, 2007.

Medina, Nestor. *Christianity, Empire and the Spirit: (Re)Configuring Faith and the Cultural*. Leiden: Brill, 2018.

Meyers, Carol, and Michael O'Connor. *The Word of the Lord Shall Go Forth*. Winona Lake, IN: Eisenbrauns, 1983.

Middleton, J. Richard. *The Liberating Image*. Grand Rapids, MI: Brazos Press, 2005.

Moo, Douglas J. *Romans: From Biblical Text to Contemporary Life*. Grand Rapids, MI: Zondervan, 2000.

————. *Galatians*. Grand Rapids, MI: Baker Academic, 2013.

————. *The Epistle to the Romans*. Grand Rapids, MI: Eerdmans, 2015.

Moore, Eddie, Ali Michael, and Marguerite W. Penick-Parks. *The Guide for White Women Who Teach Black Boys*. Thousand Oaks, CA: Corwin, 2018.

Moore, Steve. *Who Is My Neighbor?: Being a Good Samaritan in a Connected World*. Colorado Springs, CO: NavPress, 2011.

Morris, Leon. *The Gospel According to John*. Grand Rapids, MI: Eerdmans, 2008.

Mounce, Robert H. *Romans*. Nashville, TN: Broadman & Holman, 2001.

The National Mentoring Partnership and My Brother's Keeper Alliance, "Guide to Mentoring Boys and Young Men of Color," accessed October 20, 2018, https://www.mentoring.org/new-site/wp-content/uploads/2016/05/Guide-to-Mentoring-BYMOC.pdf.

Ockinga, Boyo. *Die Gottenbenbildlichkeit im Alten Agypten und im Alten Testament* [The God Image in Ancient Egypt and the Old Testament]. Wiesbaden, Germany; Harrassowitz, 1984.

Origen, *De Principiis*. Vol. 1. Peabody, MA: Hendrickson, 2012.

Ortlund, Gavin. "Image of Adam, Son of God: Genesis 5:3 and Luke 3:38 in Intercanonical Dialogue." *Journal of the Evangelical Theological Society* 57, no. 4 (2014): 673-688. Accessed September 10, 2017. ATLA Religion Database with ATLASerials. EBSCOhost.

Page, Benjamin, and Lawrence Jacobs. *Class War?: What Americans Really Think About Economic Inequity*. Chicago, IL: University of Chicago Press, 2009.

Perkins, Spencer, and Chris Rice. *More than Equals: Racial Healing for the Sake of the Gospel*. Downers Grove, IL: InterVarsity Press, 2000.

Polhill, John B. *Acts*. Vol. 26 of *The New American Commentary*. Nashville, TN: Broadman & Holman Publishers, 1992.

Potts, Donald R. "Samaria, Samaritans." In *Holman Illustrated Bible Dictionary*, edited by Chad Brand, Charles Draper, Archie England, Steve Bond, E.

Ray Clendenen, and Trent C. Butler, 1435-1437. Nashville, TN: Holman Bible Publishers, 2003.

Powell, M. A., ed. "bet, beth." *The HarperCollins Bible Dictionary*, 3rd ed. New York, NY: HarperCollins, 2011.

Powell, Mark Allan, *What Do They Hear? Bridging the Gap between Pulpit and Pew*. Nashville, TN: Abingdon, 2007.

Putnam, Robert D. *Bowling Alone: The Collapse and Revival of American Community*. New York, NY: Touchstone, 2001.

———. *Our Kids: The American Dream in Crisis*. New York, NY: Simon & Schuster, 2015.

Putnam, Robert D., Lewis M. Feldstein, and Don Cohen. *Better Together: Restoring the American Community*. London: Simon & Schuster, 2009.

Rah, Soong-Chan. *The Next Evangelicalism: Releasing the Church from Western Cultural Captivity*. Downers Grove: IVP Books, 2009.

———. *Many Colors: Cultural Intelligence for a Changing Church*. Chicago, IL: Moody Publishers, 2010.

———. *Prophetic Lament: A Call for Justice in Troubled Times*. Downers Grove, IL: IVP Books, an Imprint of InterVarsity Press, 2015.

Roop, Eugene F. *Ruth, Jonah, Esther: Believers Church Bible Commentary*. Harrisonburg, VA: Herald Press, 2002. EBSCOhost.

Rothenberg, Paula. *Race, Class, and Gender in the United States: An Integrated Study*. New York, NY: St. Martin's Press, 1995.

Salter McNeil, Brenda. *Roadmap to Reconciliation: Moving Communities into Unity, Wholeness, and Justice*. Downers Grove, IL: InterVarsity Press, 2015.

Salter McNeal, Brenda, and Rick Richardson. *The Heart of Racial Justice*. Downers Grove, IL: InterVarsity Press, 2004.

Schnabel, Eckhard J. *Acts Exegetical Commentary on the New Testament*. Grand Rapids, MI: Zondervan, 2012.

Schreiner, Thomas R. *Galatians Exegetical Commentary on the New Testament*. Grand Rapids, MI: Zondervan, 2010,

Sechrest, Love L., Johnny Ramírez-Johnson, and Amos Yong. *Can "White" People Be Saved?: Triangulating Race, Theology, and Mission*. Downers Grove, IL: IVP Academic, 2018.

Shmueli, Adi. *The Tower of Babel: Identity and Sanity*. Atlantic Highlands, NJ: Humanities Press, 1978.

Smith, David I. *On Christian Teaching: Practicing Faith in the Classroom*. Grand Rapids, MI: Eerdmans, 2018.

Smith, David I., and Barbara Carvill. *The Gift of the Stranger*. Grand Rapids, MI: Eerdmans, 2000.

Smith, David I., and Pennylyn Dykstra-Prium. *Christians and Cultural Difference*. Grand Rapids, MI: Calvin Press, 2016.

Smith, David I., and Susan M. Felch. *Teaching and Christian Imagination*. Grand Rapids, MI: Eerdmans, 2016.

Soerens, Matthew, and Jenny Hwang. *Welcoming the Stranger: Justice, Compassion & Truth in the Immigration Debate*. Downers Grove, IL: InterVarsity Press, 2018.

Songer, Harold S. "Proselytes." In *Holman Illustrated Bible Dictionary*, edited by Chad Brand, Charles Draper, Archie England, Steve Bond, E. Ray Clendenen, and Trent C. Butler, 1336. Nashville, TN: Holman Bible Publishers, 2003.

Spence-Jones H. D. M. *Exodus*. Vol. 1 of *The Pulpit Commentary*. New York, NY: Funk & Wagnalls, 1909.

Spencer, Aida Besancon. "Jesus' Treatment of Women in the Gospels." In *Discovering Biblical Equality, Complementarity without Hierarchy*, 2nd ed., edited by Ronald W. Pierce, Rebecca Merrill Groothius, and Gordon D. Fee, 126-141. Downers Grove, IL: IVP Academic, 2005.

Steinberg, Stephen. "The Long View of the Melting Pot." *Ethnic and Racial Studies* 37, no. 5 (2014): 790-794.

Strahan, Joshua Marshall. "Jesus Teaches Theological Interpretation of the Law: Reading the Good Samaritan in its Literary Context." *Journal of Theological Interpretation* 10, no. 1 (2016): 71-86.

Strauss, Mark L. *Four Portraits, One Jesus: A Survey of Jesus and the Gospels*. Grand Rapids, MI: Zondervan, 2007.

Strong, James. s.v. "*agapé* (ἀγάπη)." *The Exhaustive Concordance of the Bible*. New York, NY: Hunt and Eaton, 1894

———. s.v. "*phileó* (φιλέω)." *The Exhaustive Concordance of the Bible*. New York, NY: Hunt and Eaton, 1894.

Stuart, Douglas K. *Exodus*. Vol. 2 of *The New American Commentary*. Nashville, TN: Broadman & Holman, 2006.

Sue, Derald Wing., and David Sue. *Counseling the Culturally Diverse: Theory and Practice*, 7th ed. Hoboken, NJ: John Wiley & Sons, 2016.

Tatum, Beverly Daniel. *Why Are All the Black Kids Sitting Together in the Cafeteria?* New York, NY: Basic Books, 1997.

The National Mentoring Partnership and My Brother's Keeper Alliance. "Guide to Mentoring Boys and Young Men of Color." Accessed October 20, 2018. https://www.mentoring.org/new-site/wp-content/uploads/2016/05/Guide-to-Mentoring-BYMOC.pdf.

Thomas, Robert L. *New American Standard Hebrew-Aramaic and Greek Dictionaries: Updated Edition*. Anaheim, CA: Foundation Publications, 1998. Logos.

Thompson, Michael, Richard Ellis, and Aaron Wildavsky. *Cultural Theory*. New York, NY: Routledge, 1990.

Throntveit, Mark A. *Ezra-Nehemiah*. Louisville, KY: Westminster John Knox Press, 2012.

Turner, William Jr. "Pneumatology." In *Afro-Pentecostalism: Black Pentecostal and Charismatic Christianity in History and Culture*, edited by Amos Yong and Estrelda Y. Alexander, 169-189. New York, NY: New York University, 2011 von Rad, Gerhard. *Genesis: A Commentary*. Philadelphia, PA: Westminster, 1972.

Walton, John H. *Genesis*. Grand Rapids, MI: Zondervan, 2001.

Washington, Raleigh, and Glen Kehrein. *Breaking down Walls: A Model for Reconciliation in an Age of Racial Strife*. Chicago, IL: Moody Press, 1993.

Wattenberg, Ben. "The Melting Pot." The First Measured Century. Accessed October 12, 2018. https://www.pbs.org/fmc/timeline/emeltpot.htm.

Weaver, Gary. *Culture, Communication, and Conflict: Readings in Intercultural Relations*. Boston, MA: Pearson Publishing, 2000.

Wellman, David. *Portraits of White Racism*. New York, NY: Cambridge University Press, 1993.

Welz, Claudia. "Imago Dei." *Studia Theologica—Nordic Journal of Theology* 65, no. 1 (2011): 74-91.

Wenham, Gordon J. *The Book of Leviticus*. Grand Rapids, MI: Eerdmans, 2009.

———. *Genesis 1-15*. Grand Rapids, MI: Zondervan, 2014.

———. *Genesis 16-50*. Grand Rapids, MI: Zondervan, 2015.

West, Cornel. *Race Matters*. New York, NY: Random House, 2001.

Westbrook, Timothy Paul. "New Reflections on Mirror Neuron Research, the Tower of Babel, and Intercultural Education." *Christian Higher Education* 14, no. 5: 322-337. Accessed September 10, 2017. ATLA Religion Database with ATLASerials, EBSCOhost.

Williamson, H. G. M. *Ezra, Nehemiah*. Vol. 16 of *Word Biblical Commentary*. Waco, TX: Word, 1985.

Wright, Tom. *Paul for Everyone: Galatians and Thessalonians*. Louisville, KY: Westminster John Knox Press, 2004.

Wytsma, Ken. *The Myth of Equality: Uncovering the Roots of Injustice and Privilege*. Downers Grove, IL: IVP Books, 2017.

Yong, Amos, and Estrelda Alexander. *Afro-Pentecostalism: Black Pentecostal and Charismatic Christianity in History and Culture*. New York, NY: New York University Press, 2011.

Yong, Amos. *Hospitality and the Other: Pentecost, Christian Practices, and the Neighbor*. Maryknoll, NY: Orbis Books, 2008.

Younger, K. Lawson. *Judges, Ruth*. Vol. 6 of *The NIV Application Commentary*. Grand Rapids, MI: Zondervan Publishing House, 2002.

# About the Author

Dr. Adam Sikorski serves as Assistant Dean in the College of Church Leadership, Director of Pastoral Studies, Director of Bible Lands Studies, and Associate Professor at North Central University (NCU) in Minneapolis, Minnesota.

He holds a BA in Urban Ministries from NCU, an MA in Theological Studies and MDiv from Southwestern Assemblies of God University (SAGU), and a DMin from the Assemblies of God Theological Seminary.

Adam is an ordained AG minister, serving in vocational ministry since 1993. He served as the Director of Youth Studies at the University of Valley Forge, as an Assistant Pastor at Stone Creek Church in Urbana, IL, as an Assistant US Cohort Director for SUM Bible College and Theological Seminary, as the founder of Urbana School of Ministry, as Assistant Dean for Minnesota Teen Challenge, and over thirteen years as a youth and college/young adults pastor. His heart is to teach the next generation of ministers to go out and change the world.

In 2021, Adam became a Qualified IDI Administrator, certified to administer the Intercultural Development Inventory.

Adam and his wife, Stacy, have been married since 2002. They have two children: a daughter, Reghan, and a son, Keghan.